Like Eating Jelly with Chop Sticks

A Spiritual Journey

By Jack Narvel

For Dana Lynn - Thanks for joining us at Journey. God's blessings are raining on you. Please feel free to splash in the puddles

Phil. 4:4-7

Jack A Narvel

Copyright 2019

Scriptures marked CEV are from the Contemporary English Version of the Bible, Copyright by the American Bible Society 1991, 1992, 1995.

Scripture quotations marked ESV are taken from The ESV® Bible (The Holy Bible, English Standard Version®). ESV® Text Edition: 2016. Copyright © 2001 by Crossway, a publishing ministry of Good News Publishers. The ESV® text has been reproduced in cooperation with and by permission of Good News Publishers. All rights reserved.

Scripture marked KJV are taken from The Holy Bible, King James Version and match the 1987 printing. The KJV is public domain in the United States.

Scripture marked MSG are taken from The Message. Copyright © 1993, 1994, 1995, 1996, 2000, 2001, 2002. Used by permission of NavPress Publishing Group.

Scripture quotations marked NASB are taken from the New American Standard Bible® (NASB),Copyright© 1960, 1962, 1963, 1968, 1971, 1972, 1973,1975, 1977, 1995 by The Lockman Foundation Used by permission.

Scripture quotations marked NIV are taken from The HolyBible, New International Version. Grand Rapids: Zondervan House, 1984. Print.Used by Permission

Scripture marked NKJV are taken from the New King James Version®. Copyright © 1982 by Thomas Nelson. Used by permission. All rights reserved.

Scripture quotations marked NLT are taken from the *Holy Bible*, New Living Translation, copyright © 1996, 2004, 2015 by Tyndale House Foundation. Used by permission of Tyndale House Publishers, Inc., Carol Stream, Illinois 60188. All rights reserved.

Scripture quotations marked WEB are taken from the Web Bible (Word English Bible) available from http://ebible.org/bible/web

Table of Contents

Acknowledgements 5

Reviews 7

Introduction 11

Chapter 1 15
God's Best for All the Rest 15

Chapter 2 23
It's Christmas! Can We Open Our Gifts? 23

Chapter 3 35
The Lepers and Jesus – How Do We Say "Thank You"? 35

Chapter 4 45
The Parable of the Ten Minas - How Should I Use My Gifts? 45

Chapter 5 57
The Restaurant Owner is Looking Out for You 57

Chapter 6 91
God's Standards - Are they "Double" 91

Chapter 7 109
The Gospel of Condemnation - Why it is so popular? 109

Chapter 8 129
Christmas Expectations – How Do We Disappoint Ourselves? 129

Chapter 9 141
Disappointment with God – Who is He Really? 141

Chapter 10 151
When God Just Isn't Good Enough 151

Chapter 11 165
What Must We Do to be Saved? 165

Chapter 12 173

The Meaning of Life - A New Commandment 173
ADDITIONAL RESOURCES 188
About the Author 189

Acknowledgements

I would like to thank my friends, and fellow authors, Andy Bunch and Bob Bonnell for their help in editing and organizing this book. Also I thank them for taking the time to write their reviews.

Most of all I would like to thank my wife, Jan who has gone "above and beyond" in advising changes, creating artwork and editing this book.

I had to change the title of this book and some internal references from "Jell-O" to "Jelly" as Heinz/Kraft Foods would not allow me the use of their trademarked name "Jell-O," or "Jello" in my title or story. They made this ruling in order to protect their name from becoming "generic." I do understand their logic. It is similar to the copywriting of a book and not allowing parts to be taken out randomly and used "willy-nilly."

By using the name "Jelly" in my title and throughout this book, I am using the U.K. and European name for "gelatin." In doing so I am honoring the manufacturer's request.

Like Eating Jelly With Chop Sticks — Jack Narvel

Reviews

As I read this book, God began speaking to me on the topic of my value. He pointed out that I've had pretty good self esteem, since I know that I'm His son. However, I've not been able to articulate my value to others and I struggle to earn what I'm worth because of it. The more I've studied the value God placed inside me, who needs it, and how to supply it, the more I've grown in my understanding of my relationship with God. I didn't realize just how much I was hitting a glass ceiling in this area of my life. It's not enough to like yourself. God is bonkers, crazy for us. That level of love is what transforms us. How can we eat a doughnut or smoke a cigarette if we prize ourselves that highly, to speak nothing of the really harmful ways we abuse ourselves. This book helped me see my value from a perspective beyond myself, which is a bedrock concept if my Christian walk is to be a transformational journey.

Andy Bunch
Andy Bunch is the author of 10 books, Including, On Becoming a Man, Training the Warrior Within, Suffering Rancor, Saber and Science, Primacy of God and several anthologies.

Jack Narvel has an incredible passion for souls and a tremendous desire to communicate the gospel of God's unconditional love and of no condemnation with everyone that he meets. God's desire for creating man has always been for relationship not religion. This book in its own very unique way helps to communicate many of these truths. I am thrilled he has finally penned them down for all to see, share and glean insight. Thanks Jack, after this read none should be afraid to grab some chop sticks and dive right in! "Bon Appétit!"

Bishop Thomas Wallace II
Lead Pastor Journey Church, Myrtle Beach, SC

Jack's sense of humor through all his life and near death falls, accidents and poor choices, slapped me right across the heart! Jesus never lets up, lets go or loves us any better, or less than He did when we were little kids.

Jack says he was a Hippie in California in the 70's. He tells us about a restaurant in San Francisco, where the owner and staff made their guests feel alive by kicking them verbally in the shins or elsewhere. But he learned from that experience that God loves us, even when others don't.

Are we to believe that Jack is the only one who has stumbled through this "Christian life," looking for God when He is already in us? While totally unaware, himself, Jack kept angels and others, fully employed rescuing, providing and assisting, as God reached out.

In this book you can hitch a ride in the backseat of Jack's 1990 Dodge Dakota riding across the country and around the world. You will discover how eating a banquet meal with God and

Moses on Mt. Sinai is much more exciting than trying to dine on Jelly with chop sticks in San Francisco.

Jack, my brother, this has been one of the best rides of my life. Thank you for helping me to know how much Jesus loves me 24/7 365 with or without my permission! Mostly the latter!

Bob Bonnell
Bob is Pastor of Communion Fire Church in Myrtle Beach and the Author of
Be Bold. Believe. The Miracle of Communion Fire
Copyright 2018, Christian Faith Publishing

Jack Narvel has an incredible passion for souls and a tremendous desire to communicate the gospel of God's unconditional love and of no condemnation with everyone that he meets. God's desire for creating man has always been for relationship not religion. This book in its own very unique way helps to communicate many of these truths.

Rick Sarver
Pastor Rick Sarver is Co- Pastor of Grace Life Fellowship Chuch in Myrtle Beach, SC. Rick is the author of **I'm Saved - Now What?**
Rick along with his wife DeAnn are also proprietors of the Boardwalk Coffee House located at 104 9th Ave N.
In Myrtle Beach which offers both great food and wonderful coffee creations all year.

Like Eating Jelly With Chop Sticks   Jack Narvel

Introduction

If you are curious about my title, there is an annual contest to see who can eat the most "Jelly," or gelatin dessert, with chop sticks. It's kind of like the hot dog eating contest that Nathan's Hot Dogs does in New York City every year. There are prizes, I hope … (there must be?) There is a current Guinness World Record for how many grams of Jelly were eaten in one minute. The record is held by a German man named Andre Ortlof, who ate 716 grams or 1.57 pounds of "Jelly" using chop sticks in one minute.

Why would anyone WANT to eat "Jelly" with chop sticks? I think anyone in his or her right mind would want to know. Eating "Jelly" with chop-sticks is difficult even if it was cut into little squares (which it can't be for the Guinness record). I have tried it myself. It is not easy. It is more trouble than it's worth unless you are REALLY into silly contests. And/or you want to achieve minor fame by getting your name in the Guinness Book of World Records. The current "Jelly with chop sticks champion," Andre, tried several times before actually beating the world record in February of 2017. This Jelly eating record breaking will not be easy. Andre's record still stands. So maybe the rest of us should continue to eat "Jelly" with a spoon!

That's the background for the title, but the real purpose for this book is to understand how and why people, particularly Christians, make life more difficult for themselves than it has to be. Why is it, when God thinks we are so valuable that He gave His only Son that we might spend this life and eternity with Him, that so many pursue lives of self-deprecation? Why is it that when God says we are "Perfect and Holy" are we inclined to disagree with Him?

Like Eating Jelly With Chop Sticks

Jack Narvel

The inspiration for this lifestyle paradox comes, not from eating "Jelly" with chop sticks, but from a small Chinese Restaurant in San Francisco, Chinatown in the 1970s.

Today, when I go into a Chinese Restaurant, I expect a certain level of cleanliness and care. The tablecloths should be red or perhaps white vinyl. They should have been wiped down recently and there should be no spilled food visible on the floor, under or around the table. The help at a Chinese Restaurant is generally "family" so they can be expected to perform well for the mom and dad or the aunt and uncle who own the place.

Back then, when I was a Hippie musician in the '70s in San Francisco, there was an exception to this "Familial Chinese Restaurant rule." It was called Sam Wo's Restaurant. Sam's was a three-story edifice located at 813 Washington Street which remained in that spot for many years until the restaurant was closed by the Health Department in 2012, due to health code violations (Ratatouille was apparently helping prepare food in the kitchen). They have since re-opened and relocated to Clay Street.

In the '70s, we "counter-culture sorts," were all looking for a unique dining experience and Sam Wo's was just the ticket! It was a narrow building with three flights of narrow stairs that led to dining rooms on the second and third floors. The kitchen was on the first floor with "dumb waiters" (no pun intended) which would transport the food to the dining rooms.

Sam's was unique among Chinese restaurants in that it did not serve fortune cookies. I think that exclusion was instituted by Sam's because so many regulars were gifted in the prophetic. The cookies would have been an unnecessary duplication of function.

The main drawing card at Sam's was a waiter named "Edsel Ford Fung (Fong)." He specialized in cursing customers in Chinese and English. Legend has it that he would not even serve customers whose appearance he didn't like. Edsel passed in 1984 and was memorialized, in the San Francisco Chronicle, by the iconic columnist: Herb Caen. Edsel was also memorialized by having his portrait painted on the "Gold Mountain Mural," near the restaurant, which depicted famous Chinese characters in American History. Pretty special for a guy who made his fame by insulting and ignoring customers. Edsel would summarily welcome diners, who lingered by the stairs to his third-floor abode, by curtly saying: "Sit down and shut up!"

Aside from his uniqueness among Chinese restaurant employees (he was also a part-owner) was that he would say to people, who asked for a knife and fork: "No knife, no fork! You eat with chop sticks like real person!" He became an international celebrity. Was his pique an act? Was he really angry all the time? We may never know for sure until we get to Heaven. Imagine meeting Edsel Ford Fong there next to St. Peter at the "other" Golden Gate.

So with Edsel's pejorative command ("Sit down, Shut up!") in mind, I welcome you to the world of Jelly and Chop Sticks.

Like Eating Jelly With Chop Sticks   Jack Narvel

Chapter 1

God's Best for All the Rest

As you read on, you may wonder why so many people came to Sam Wo's? Was it just to be insulted by Edsel; or was it something else? The noodles were good, but they were just noodles. The "ambiance" was "early trailer park." The restaurant itself was small and cramped, with small tables and, usually, with a long waiting line down the stairs.

I once took one of my customers and his wife, who were visiting San Francisco, to Sam Wo's. I told them about the "Famous Edsel Ford Fong." Upon being seated in the third-floor dining area, both he and his wife were summarily insulted by Edsel. My customer who was a psychologist, should have known the reason, but, none-the-less asked: "Why would anyone want to eat here?" I was momentarily speechless. But quite obviously, being from the Midwest, my customer was not able to appreciate the "ambiance" of a small unkempt Chinese noodle restaurant with an unkempt and insulting (but famous) waiter. There are, of course, many reasons why a person would choose to dine at Sam Wo's. I had no easy answer, for my clients, but that experience is the inspiration for this book.

The fame and fortune of Sam Wo's does boggle the mind. We were all hippies, even the businessmen, looking for a unique experience to get ourselves a bigger "charge" out of our otherwise dull and un-provoking lives. Yes, that must have been it! The fame of Edsel Ford Fong and the restaurant itself was evidence of the larger "gestalt." It was a mere moment in time, which underscored the values of a generation. All the powers of the universe had come together in that instant, in that location, to create the experience all San Franciscans had been longing for, secretly, in their heart of hearts… a waiter who agreed with them that "they were without value!"

But, right now, in our present-day culture (which has grown beyond sitting in a bookstore smoking pot and seeking "true enlightenment" from Alan Ginsburg's poetry and Jack Kerouac's novels), you may be asking yourself; Why does anyone like to go to places like Sam Wo's? Is it because it is "famous"? Is it because you might meet a "celebrity" there? Various Hollywood personalities could be seen there. Herb Caen, The San Francisco Examiner columnist, was a regular. I never met him. I never even asked anyone for an autograph….sigh. Edsel would have probably thrown me out if he saw that I was seeking autographs. My wife Jan was also taken there when she was fourteen by her older brothers. She was fortunate that Edsel did not try to assault her, as he was sometimes known to do.

However, lest we think Sam's Wo's was simply an artifact of the "Beat Generation," why, even here in Myrtle Beach (a "family friendly resort"), there is a restaurant called "Dick's Last Resort." When you go to Dick's, the staff intentionally insult you and offer you large paper cook's hats with rude things drawn on them. Customer reviews say that the food is excellent and the portions are decent. They even note that the wait staff "will leave you alone if you ask them to." One customer wrote: "But why would you? The goodhearted insults are part of the experience."

That is all wonderful, I suppose if you actually travel somewhere and are expecting to be insulted. But what about those situations when you feel abused, insulted and you were not expecting it? Yes, as we all know, there are those experiences, too.

For instance, I had a bad experience at a Home Improvement store over Easter weekend. I reacted badly to the checkout clerk telling me I could no longer have the serviceman's discount that I was used to getting as a Veteran. All I had to do was show my service I.D. Card and ten percent would be taken off my bill.

BUT, she said, "The store has changed its policy two months ago. You will need to have a store Identification Card to get your discount at checkout now, sir. You can go 'on-line' and order one." …You can imagine my delight at being informed the store was in the process of making it "easier to check out" and get my discount. Particularly as I was already standing in the checkout line at the time! It had been a long wait in line already, because of the Easter crowds gathered to obtain their "Garden Bunny Figurines" and decorative flags.

But to the clerk's mind, I would only have to be momentarily inconvenienced today, in order to experience new and improved benefits tomorrow.

But there was my point of view, which I felt should be taken under consideration. Instead of taking advantage of the relatively simple process, where I simply showed my military I.D. card at checkout to receive my ten percent discount, the game had been changed. Now, in order to transact my usual business with them, I have to have a store I.D. card. Which card, I would I have to take the time to apply for and fill out online. From the store's point of view, the store would now have a convenient record of all my purchases This record would both benefit their marketing department, as well as benefit me, if ever I needed to return something without a receipt. But that would not be the case today, No Sir!

The clerk was very helpful, as my internal anger continued to rise. She said I could go elsewhere in the store, stand in another line to get a card. At that counter, I could even have the customer service person fill out the card application for me, online, right there at the store. What could be more convenient? Then, I could go back, and pick up my cart, stand in line again, and check out with my new and improved card.

Did I wish to pursue either of these options on the Saturday afternoon before Easter, or did I prefer to get angry, abandon my cart at the checkout and tell them what I thought of their "new store policy" in no uncertain terms? Right you are! I said I was "headed for another store: where I could get the same merchandise AND receive the kind of treatment I believe I deserve as a veteran!"

As I drove away, I repented of my bad attitude about a half-hour later. I felt embarrassed and humbled that I had vented my self-righteous anger at two employees who had no part in the making of the new store policy. It was also Easter weekend, when we remember Christ's sacrifice for us and how we, as Christians, are supposed to behave as He did (at least in public). I called my Pastor and confessed I had lost control and vented at two innocent parties. If we were Catholic, I could have said "Forgive me, Father, for I have sinned" and received absolution. But being under Grace, not Law, I am already forgiven at the "God-Man" level and all I needed to do was correct the offense at the "Man-Man" level. So my Pastor suggested I drive back to the store and apologize.

On the surface of it, driving back to apologize would have been a righteous and sensible solution. I considered pursuing that path. I even believe I would have …. But, the store was a half-hour drive from where I was located at that time. It was on a very busy road and it would have taken more than an hour of my time to make the round trip.

I was almost ready to go back anyway and "do the right thing"… until… just as I was leaving Walmart, I overheard two employees talking. The one woman was saying to the other, "I've worked retail for fifteen years and I have NEVER been insulted by a customer before today. It was so much fun!"

I decided that if that were the case with the Walmart employee, perhaps I had inadvertently "made someone's day" at the Home Improvement store! What a blessing in disguise I must have been. I continued to the parking lot and made my way home.

Most of the time, when I have been insulted, even in good humor, it has not sat well with me. Perhaps, because I was not as certain, then, of who I was in Christ, as I am today. There is an issue here with which we all, saved or unsaved, need to deal at some point in our lives. For those of us who recognize that we are saved by Grace, not by works, we still seem to forget from time to time what it means to be God's son or daughter. What does it mean that we are the very brother, or sister of Christ? The Bible even says that we believers are "raised up with Him and seated with Him in the Heavenly places in Christ Jesus"(Eph 2:6 ESV) not "someday," but right now!

Am I worthy of God's Love but not Man's love? Am I even worthy of God's love? These questions occur to all of us, sooner or later. Sometimes, they are unresolved throughout our lives.

Consider this: there's a story in the Bible about a Leper who wasn't sure if he could qualify for healing? The leper wasn't sure if he was "good enough." for Jesus to heal him.

"And behold a leper came to Him and knelt before Him saying, 'Lord, if you will, you can make me clean'. And Jesus stretched out His hand and touched him saying,'I will; be clean'.And immediately his leprosy was cleansed." (Matthew 8:2-3.ESV)

The Leper believed Jesus COULD heal him. He had heard of the many miraculous signs Jesus had performed. But the lepers of that day were outcast. They had to shout "Unclean! Unclean!" Whenever they walked near uninfected people. How could such a person, with no self-respect at all, feel he was worthy for the Son of Man, the Son of God to even look at him, much less heal him, much less TOUCH him! WOW!

The question begs repeating, am I like the leper? Do I consider myself unworthy? This is question we will cover in more detail, as this book continues.

But let's go back to San Francisco for a moment.Were we, the patrons of Sam Wo's, so unsure of our true identity that we would feel comfortable only in a place where our own self-image was validated by the curses and slights of "a person of authority," this Edsel Ford Fong? If I am truly as worthless as I may think I am, maybe I should eat in a place where others will agree with me."Hopeless wretch that I am."

Sociometric studies have shown that people love to have their opinions confirmed by others, "for the sense of self-worth that it gives them." Perhaps you can see the irony here.

Speaking of personal identity and insulting waiters… is a person who has a certainty of "who they are in Christ" less likely to seek out insults? Or would such a person who is secure in their identity be more likely to seek out insults "just for the fun of it"?

Something to be studiously pondered, as we dutifully consider the possibility of a thundershower tomorrow.

I certainly know we can withstand insults more readily when we are clear about who we are in Christ. We don't need to have an identity crisis in the shop. But should we seek difficult people out, even for intentional fun? We will examine these paradoxical truths and questions as we move further along. But for now, let's have a good time and celebrate Christmas!

Like Eating Jelly With Chop Sticks   Jack Narvel

Chapter 2

It's Christmas! Can We Open Our Gifts?

Like a child at Christmas, if you came from a solidly middle-class family, as I did, you would wish for certain gifts well before Christmas. If you had parents that indulged you, they would take you shopping before Christmas. They would notice, without telling you, what you were really spending time looking at. They might say things like: "Oh that's too expensive for us. I see you like it, Honey, but we can't afford that this year." Alternatively, if you were under six years of age (probably the top age for kids to stop believing in Santa Claus), your parents might say: "Let's put that on a list of things we want from Santa." Notice the use of the word "we." They used the word "we" because at your tender age, your parents wanted you to know that they, too, believed in Santa. By implication, they were saying that they would also expect his gifts.

Santa was the ultimate gift giver. He had little or no concern for a budget. He could bring you the biggest and the best, whether it was a huge stuffed toy from F.A.O. Schwartz, all the way from New York City, or the most fantastic Huffy Bicycle with flying plastic streamers attached to the holes in the shiny plastic handles at the end of the handlebars. Even before you ever rode it, you could imagine the wind in your hair and the streamers blowing out beside you as you glided downhill, at what would be close to 50 miles an hour! You were risking life and limb, but who cared? Santa had made the Bike, and me indestructible! There are motorcycle riders today who so believe that "they are indestructible" that they know they have no need to wear a helmet, or protective clothing of any kind. I see them riding on the Interstate at 50-60 miles per hour with nothing but a T-shirt and shorts! Perhaps they are trusting the fact that God made them, and their Bike, and that both are "Pretty darn near indestructible!" Ah well. But let's get back to my Christmas story.

Bicycles, large stuffed toys, and electric train sets! Yes, these were the fine gifts that Santa brought. I can still remember my fifth birthday. My birthday is on the 23rd of December, so I seldom got both birthday gifts AND Christmas gifts, except from my parents. Of course, Santa would always remember me on Christmas Day.

On the morning of Christmas Day, after my fifth birthday, I walked down the stairs from the third floor, past my grandma's and grandpa's bedrooms on the second floor to the top of the stairs looking down between the bannisters to the first floor. Through the railings, I could see the Christmas Tree with the electric train set up on the board below it. There was a little village with artificial snow and then, and then… I saw it! It was the largest stuffed toy elephant I had ever seen. I ran back up the stairs yelling: "Mommy, Mommy, Santa brought me an elephant!"

"No honey," she said, "that couldn't be. An elephant would never fit in our living room." But I insisted: "No Mommy, not a **REAL** elephant, but the biggest stuffed elephant I've ever seen!" So dutifully, she got out of bed. She put on her robe and slippers. and came downstairs to see the largest stuffed elephant she had ever seen. "Oh, my" she exclaimed, "I never have seen anything so big!"

But, of course, she HAD seen it before. She bought it for me at F.A.O. Schwartz in New York City. How she was able to smuggle it back from our annual trip to New York, I have no idea. This

Like Eating Jelly With Chop Sticks   Jack Narvel

was 1949, long before "online shopping" made it possible to conceal a myriad of things from the prying eyes of children at Christmas. There were "Christmas Catalogs" from the larger department and clothing stores, and one could order gifts through the mail. But shopping by mail was not nearly as convenient then, as Amazon has made shopping by internet today.

Parents can now "go online," rather than having "incriminating catalogs" lying about for the children to see. The gifts delivered are delivered in plain brown cardboard boxes with only the word "Amazon" printed outside. One would not know whether there was a toy or a carton of fruit jam inside. There was no clue as to its place of origin.

It's no wonder why in "the season to be jolly" that Toys 'R Us is closing stores. The crowds are simply too large. The checkout lines are inconvenient and trying to find a clerk to help you find what you are seeking can be an exercise in futility at best. It is so much easier and less disruptive to our busy lives to shop online.

Now, I promise, "no more rabbit trailing"! Let's go back to the Christmas of the year I turned five. I imagine now that the elephant must have arrived on the porch in a box. The box would have been marked in large type "F.A.O Schwartz, New York, N.Y." Fortunately, my Grandma lived at home and could intercept any mail, without it being detected by others.

Being a parent myself, I get that part of the fun of Christmas is to hide gifts from the kids, hoping against hope the children will not stand on a chair and reach way back into the dark reaches of the closet (which no one ever uses) to find a wrapped gift. (Oh Joy!) And then to attempt to figure out a way to unwrap the gift and see what it is (experiencing great joy, or deep sorrow, depending…)

Finally, the child is able to discover a way to wrap and tape the gift back up again to make it look undisturbed. (NOT!) The child must not have torn the wrapping or left tape marks on the wrap where the tape had formerly been. The child should go through all this effort to cover his, or her, crime of inquisitiveness, because, in the child's heart of hearts, the child would never want to spoil its parents joy on Christmas morning when they too, along with all of us, could experience the surprise of the unexpected gifts we had received from Santa.

When we lived in Illinois, we were just getting established as a family of four adopted kids and two parents. We bought an old enclosed 4x4 "Nationwide" utility trailer. It could be used for hauling things to the dump, helping neighbors move, or …to hide things! It was lockable and concealed gifts of all sizes (even the bicycle in pieces that had to be assembled overnight before Christmas Day)

Well, as you may have thought, God does this very thing as well, even without a trailer or a closet. He gives us wonderful gifts, which may well be beyond our expectations, and not just at Christmas. In Proverbs, we are told, "It is the Glory of God to conceal a matter, but the honor of kings to search out a matter." (Proverbs 25:2.KJV) Gifts from God are often not physical, but supernatural. God has the power and the desire to create occasions, with "gifts" (yes, even more than one), which we will remember for the rest of our lives.

James in the Bible was Jesus' half brother. He writes, "Whatever is good and perfect is a gift coming down to us from God our Father, who created all the lights in the Heavens. He never changes or casts a shifting shadow." (James 1:17.NLT) This is a promise from God, to us, that we will receive not only good gifts, not even great gifts, but "perfect gifts." And not just at Christmas, but anytime. And, without even taking us shopping, God knows just what is just right for each of us.

Now, you may ask, "How does God know what is the perfect gift for me?" Well, the answer to that question is simple. He created us, He is eternal. He lives outside of time. He has already seen our entire life pass before His eyes. "For I know the plans I have for you, declares the Lord, plans to prosper you and not to harm you, plans to give you hope and a future."(Jeremiah 29:11.NIV) We need to "just believe," not in Santa, but just believe that The Lord has good plans for us, even when, or especially when, times are tough.

Within that plan and purpose, God has planned gifts. These are not just the gifts of the Spirit, which are detailed in Romans 12:7-11, but also physical gifts in our bodies, which can suddenly manifest (such as healing), or even "Earthly Physical Gifts" like cars. These gifts, physical or even spiritual, are not usually manifest instantaneously and out of nowhere, but I have personally seen unexpected gifts such as cars, televisions, beds, and even cash come to us in times of need. They were given through the hands of those whom God has appointed.

In fact, our only vehicle, when we came back from a mission trip to Australia, was a 1990 Dodge Dakota pick up truck, given to us by a family in Washington State. Our next assignment was YWAM Myrtle Beach and we had no vehicle to use when we got there. We also had not much in the way of personal possessions after three years as missionaries in Australia. We had parked Jan's sewing fabrics and sewing machine at a friend's shop. We had no tables, lamps, chairs or even a bed to sleep in. We apprised our friends at church of our needs. We went to some garage sales and fundraisers. The result was a two-thirds full, sixteen-foot moving truck! I felt like the Israelites must have felt leaving town after having "plundered the Egyptians" on the way to the Holy Land. So off we went towing the pick up truck with 150,000 miles on it, behind our Ryder Truck, full of our new (to us) stuff.

That 1990 Dodge Dakota pick up, was more than a miracle gift to us for our transportation in our new assignment. It was also given to increase our faith. After a year, in Myrtle Beach, the transmission failed! It would not come out of Second Gear.

We took it to a local transmission shop, run by a Brother in Christ. He told us we needed a new transmission. Even a used one was beyond our Social Security and mission donor income. Given our financial inflexibility, the owner's wife suggested the owner and I pray over the vehicle. We did and the transmission was immediately restored to "like-new condition." We never had to have it serviced again. Praising God with my family and friends at Church for this "miracle story."

But, after another year, the transmission, again, exhibited the same symptoms. It would not leave second gear. This time, I prayed over it personally, as I was driving to a nearby shopping center. It stopped dead at the main intersection. I prayed again, hit the ignition and it immediately started again, with no further difficulties. Much praising of God and thankfulness ensued.

After another year, the transmission appeared stuck again in second gear as I drove it to the dump with a YWAM friend. We laid hands on the dashboard. We declared how the truck "was donated to the use of God's purposes, and that the devil had no right to it! Hands off this truck, devil!

As we stopped at a traffic light, I looked down at the gearshift lever and the truck was in "2," second gear! The lesson I learned from this incident is that we all have the power of healing within us. There are some folks who have God-given attributes which make them more likely to be aware of certain issues than others. The Transmission specialist was expert in applying the skills God had given him, to transmissions in the natural. He also had confidence in the supernatural power God gives us to be able to pronounce divine healing, much as Jesus did.

The use of such persons in human affairs is a blessing. But what God showed me the second time I was stuck in "2," was that I owned the truck, and as such, it was my job to declare the blessing over it. I declared the blessing, and it worked again. The third time, I was reminded of God's sense of humor. As we do the "wrong thing," when we err in life, those errors have consequences. When we shift the lever into second and assume the gears will automatically shift, as they would if it were in "D," we are banking on God breaking His own physical laws to rectify our stupidity. He can do that, but He seldom does. He would prefer we learn from our own mistakes. God's miracles, while they may benefit us directly, are not to puff us up with self-importance. Rather they are always done to the "Glory of God". It is His name, not our name which is lifted up in the process!

Four years later the engine gave out, due to a burst head gasket. While we might have successfully prayed for the "head gasket" to be restored, we sold it to the "recycle yard" instead.

"Oh ye of little faith," the Lord might have chided us, but since we both were working in the same location, we seldom needed a second vehicle on which we would pay taxes and insurance. Sometimes you just have to let things go. Even Lazarus died a second time.

Sometimes, we get unexpected gifts, as I have noted, above. Just when we are feeling content with our lot in life. The Holy Spirit is both willing and able to touch others to impart gifts to share with us. As King David writes, "Delight yourself in the Lord and He will give you the desires of your heart."(Psalm 37:4.NASB) And, why not? When we are believers following the Holy Spirit that lives within us, it could rightly be said that God Himself even puts these desires in our hearts.

I was born in December of 1944. I can recall many of the physical gifts which God has used others to give to me. In a perfect world, and in my own mind, I would like to know all the gifts God has for me which are yet to come in life. If I could peek into a crystal ball, or open a closet door, I'd like to know. But, like the boy standing on the chair in the closet, it would not feel right, at my age, to spoil the surprise!

God says that it is His delight to conceal or hide things from us so that we will experience the joy of the search, the exploration, the journey, to find what He had in mind for us all along. Need I remind you again that,"It is the Glory of God to conceal a matter, but the glory of kings to search out a matter?" (Proverbs 25:2.NASB)

It's not just on Christmas morning, but at any time or any place, God has a series of surprises just for us! Graham Cooke calls these surprises "suddenlies." We suddenly realize the value of what we have been seeking, consciously or unconsciously, all along; just as suddenly we receive it! What a wonderful Father is our God!

Speaking of Christmas gift lists, God seems to say, "go ahead, make out a list and share it with me." In Psalm 37, God says he will "… give you the desires of your heart." He adds in the next verse," Commit your way to the Lord, trust also in Him and He will bring it to pass." (Psalm 37:4-5.NKJV)

Now, just think about that for a minute … of course He will give you the desires of your heart. He put those desires in your heart through His Holy Spirit when you became a believer. He wants you to have all those good and perfect gifts that are found in His Heavenly "F.A.O. Schwartz Toy Store." All I have to do is trust in Him to be my provider. I don't have to buy lottery tickets, I don't have to start a "Go Fund Me Page" on Facebook. When I simply trust in God to provide, then I will receive the desires of my heart, even without asking.

Of course, I **do** need to be willing to receive those gifts. I can't be spending my time and thoughts on "I wish I may, I wish I might, have the million dollars I wish for tonight." I also can't be ruminating on the thought: "Am I really good enough for God?" Well, the answer is really simple, that before you have Jesus: **"of course you're not good enough for God"** That's why the Father sent His Son, Jesus, so we could have the righteousness of Christ in us. God took our sins away through Jesus, "He made Him who knew no sin to be sin on our behalf, so that we might become the righteousness of God in Him" (2 Corinthians 5:21.NASB)

After we have Jesus living in us, we then **are** worthy, we have His Glory and we have His Spirit living in us. We are "His righteousness" because, as believers, we have Him in us. Every day can be Christmas morning when we wake up in the expectation that we are "good enough." We are children of the King; we are full of His righteousness; we are excited to see what adventure Daddy God has for us today.

In the words of the song: "Or would you like to swing on a star, carry moonbeams home in a jar, and be better off than you are, or would you rather be a mule?" ("Swingin' on a Star" by Burke and VanHeusen)

Some Christians, it seems, would rather not experience the lavish love of God, but would rather eat noodles and be sworn at by Chinese waiters. Or maybe they would even believe to be reincarnated as a mule where they could reluctantly be "beaten into service."Hopefully not us!

Like Eating Jelly With Chop Sticks   Jack Narvel

Chapter 3

The Lepers and Jesus – How Do We Say "Thank You"?

With these stories in mind, it may occur to you to ask, "Why do I settle for less than God's best in my life, in general?" Why do I seek out difficult people? If I feel I am unworthy, then, naturally, I will seek to confirm this self-assessment in my interactions with others. On the other hand, if I consider myself a "Good Joe," intelligent, good looking and the life of any party, I should seek out confirmation of that self-image. That's just what social research tells us. We tend to seek out experiences and even news articles which confirm our opinions, both of ourselves and particularly of the world in general.

Can we achieve that level of self-worth, self-confidence and even bravery in today's world to speak out and act out against social injustice? More importantly, can we be motivated to defend our faith at a time when Christianity is challenged worldwide?

The state of the world today reminds me of what we used to say in the '60s when someone objected to the music or person of Elvis Presley, "Can one million Elvis fans be wrong?" The phrase implied that we should "get on the bandwagon" and see the value in what so many others cherished, regardless of whether or not we agreed.

The ultimate value in our lives is not in how well we agree with a majority, rather it's believing in the value we have to others, and to God. Not as a trend follower, not as a party member, not because of our social status, but for the very gifts God has given us to use, with, and for others.

Let's look at the value of self-image for a group of people who in Bible times were the bottom of the social barrel. Their bodies were literally rotting away with leprosy. No one wanted to touch them, or even go near them. No hugs, for them, not even at church. In fact, they weren't allowed in church. They couldn't go to the altar to be prayed for and receive healing. They had to live outside the city. If they ever ran into another human being they had to cry out "Unclean, Unclean!" A very demeaning state of mind and body, no doubt about it. What would their self-image have been? I've already given a short burst of the "lone leper" story in the Chapter One.

And now, there is the story of the ten lepers in Luke 17, "As He entered a village He was met by ten lepers, who stood at a distance and lifted upon their voices, saying,' Jesus, Master have mercy on us'." Jesus didn't even touch the ten. He just told them to "go to the priests and show yourselves." (Luke 17:11-19.ESV)

Of course, all ten were healed. The priests would not come to them. There was no "Leper Colony Outreach." Once the lepers were healed (miraculously), then they were to show themselves to the Priests to be examined and pronounced healthy. They knew what Jesus was implying when He told them to go to the Priests. They knew that healing must be at hand.

This story in Luke tells us that only one came back to give thanks to the Man who spoke healing over him. And he was a Samaritan, an enemy of the Jews. Interestingly, Jesus never said to the leper who came back: "Oh yeah, thanks, it was, after all, **my** power which healed you." He could have said,"You're a

Samaritan **and** a leper. You should be thankful that I even spoke to you."Rather, Jesus said, "Rise up and go your way; your **Faith** has made you well."(Luke 17:19.ESV)

It was the **fear** of the lepers which caused them to shout to Jesus from a distance. It was the **faith** of the lepers which caused them to cry out to Jesus before He reached out to them. It was their faith in Jesus to obey His command to go to the Temple and show the priests that you are healed, even before that healing was manifest in their bodies. It was their faith in Jesus, that even as they walked they must have begun to notice their sores were healing. Bones and fingers were being restored! What an amazing moment that must have been for all of them. But only one came back to thank Jesus for manifesting that healing within them.

It is interesting to me that only one of the ten came back and threw himself at Jesus' feet, thanking Him for His healing. The Bible says "and he was a Samaritan." The Samaritans were the enemies of the Jews, so a Samaritan would have to be very bold and full of faith to approach Jesus (the Jewish Rabbi) and request healing. That may be why they "stood at a distance" and said, "Master have mercy on us." For the one Samaritan to approach Jesus, after he was healed, would have been a huge step of faith. After all, he might have thought "I am still not worthy to approach this man." The Law of Moses says a leper is **not** officially healed until a Priest confirms the healing by careful examination. (Leviticus 14:3-8.ESV). These ten were on their way to the Priests, they had not yet been declared "healed."

Jesus clarifies the healing process both then and now, because He is our new High Priest. Jesus' authority to heal and cleanse exceeds that of any Levitical Priest. He still heals through us and in us today!

After the Samaritan leper returns to thank Him, Jesus declares, "Your faith has healed you."(Luke17:19.ESV)

Do we have that kind of faith today?

Now, let's go back to Matthew to look at the story of the single leper. This is one of my favorite Bible stories. It's about a man with leprosy, who trusted God enough to actually approach Jesus and ask for healing. The way in which he asks is what distinguishes this story. Unlike the ten lepers, shouting from a distance, as described in Luke, this leper approached Jesus in person, albeit gingerly. He **did know** that he was a leper. He should be shouting "Unclean, Unclean!" All "civilized lepers" would have. Jesus and his disciples should have rejected him.

From the leper's point of view, he must have committed some awful sin which had caused him to become struck with leprosy in the first place. He knew Jesus COULD heal him. He believed Jesus had the power to forgive, whatever sin had caused leprosy to manifest. His question would have been, "is the Son of God WILLING to literally step down and heal me?" Here's how the encounter reads in Matthew 8.

"Suddenly a man with leprosy approached him and knelt before Him. 'Lord', the man said, 'if you are willing you can heal me and make me clean.'" (Matthew 8:2-3.CEV) It's amazing, that in that time and in that culture, this leper would be bold enough to ask Jesus personally for a favor of this magnitude. Leprosy was not a random illness, but rather caused by his own personal sin. Yet "Jesus reached out His hand and touched the man. 'I am willing.' He said, 'Be clean!' Immediately, he was cleansed of his leprosy."(Matt 8:2-4,NIV)

It is of note that the leprous man's appearance and doubtless, body odor, would have been most offensive and any "normal" person would have healed him first and embraced him later, if at all. Yet, Jesus actually "touched him" first, **before** healing him.

The lesson in this story is that this one was actively seeking a personal relationship with the Son of God. The ten, on the other hand, were just wanting to be "leprosy free."

Jesus actually touched this one man to confirm His love for him. Unlike the ten lepers who were healed, as they walked away, this man was healed instantly. Instant healing is always an unexpected gift.

That question of the leper in Matthew 8, might apply today for all of us. We need not ask, as believers: "Lord, are you willing?" Nor should we say "Jesus, Master, have mercy on us." After Jesus death and Ressurection, He bled and died for all our sickness all our infirmities. The Word says, "He was pierced for our transgressions, He was crushed for our iniquities; the punishment which brought us peace was on Him and by His wounds we are healed."(Isaiah 53:5.NIV This passage from Isaiah 53:5 repeats in 1 Peter 2:24. Rather, we can say in faith "Lord, I am willing to receive all that you have for me." "I am willing to accept your suffering and sacrifice for me, 'once and for all.'"

The title of this book begs the question, "Am I O.K. to approach and fellowship with Jesus as I am, or do I think I should be spending a whole lot more energy and effort in order to be good enough to receive God's grace?

I remember the old hymn the chorus would sing at the Billy Graham Crusades, "Just as I am, I come, I come." Still today, after all those Billy Graham Crusades, believers may still ask, "Am I sick, because I am cursed by God for something I did or did not do?" That's how the Hebrews felt about Leprosy. We still have leprosy in some places today, but now the medical community refers to it as "Hansen's Disease." According to WebMD.com, in 2019 there are still in excess of 2,610 active cases of Hansen's Disease. That represents a significant increase over the 107 that were noted by the World Health Organization in 2015. Its cause is a slow-growing type of bacteria which may take up to TWENTY YEARS between exposure to the bacteria the development of symptoms.

You can see where the ancients might have seen it as a curse from God, as there was no immediate connection between exposure and symptomatic manifestation.

Like the one leper of the ten, who knelt before Jesus, or the one leper who boldly approached the "throne of Grace" personally, do any of us today have the firm belief that Jesus **is** the one? Do we have the faith to trust in him for what we need?

The disciples of John the Baptist asked Jesus in Matthew,"Are you the Messiah, we've been expecting or should we keep looking for someone else?"(Matthew 11:3.NLT) John the Baptist had told them to ask Jesus this question. Yet, John was Jesus cousin. We are told in the book of Luke that when Jesus and John were yet unborn, Mary went to visit her cousin Elizabeth. while both were pregnant. Elizabeth was carrying the last prophet of the Old Testament (John), and Mary was carrying Jesus, the Messiah (or the first Rabbi of the New Testament, The Promised One)."When Elizabeth heard Mary's greeting, the baby leaped in her womb." (Luke 1:41.NASB) Two beings, yet unborn, so connected in the Spirit that they would react physically to each other's presence.

Later, John even baptized Jesus in the River Jordan as "The Lamb of God, who takes away the sin of the world," (John 1:29.ESV). Jesus would be sacrificed for the sins of a Nation. John knew that was His purpose, yet John now doubted Jesus' identity. John expected Jesus, as God, to release him from prison and punish Herod for his crimes. John was thinking carnally, that if Jesus really was the Son of God, then Jesus would surely rescue his cousin and Herod should be killed with Jesus' "mighty sword of truth." John knew Jesus had the power. Of course he would use it. Why wouldn't He? (See more of this line of thought about "expectations" in Chapter 8.)

Regardless of John's expectations in later life, that story of two beings in their mother's wombs reacting to each other gives a whole different perspective as to "when life begins" and whether or not abortion is murder. That is an adventure in meditation for another time.

For now, I continue examine whether I think, in my heart of hearts, that somehow,"I do not deserve God's best for me." Even John the Baptist in prison wasn't too sure of who he was. John was convinced that because he had done or not done something as God intended that he was being punished and would be killed by men, absent Jesus Divine Intervention.

Do we see **ourselves** in the words of the hymn, Amazing Grace, "…how sweet the sound that saved a wretch like me?" I guess I am "a wretch," I deserve nothing but death. I don't understand why God would send a Savior for me. I am undeserving of God's banquet table. I deserve to eat fast food in small crowded spaces and be insulted… "sorry wretch that I am."

Is that why we seek out demeaning experiences? Is that why we fall into drugs, alcohol, illicit sex, even an overindulgence in food, so that we can somehow prove to ourselves that after all, we are not worthy of the love of our King, and we never have been? Is that the root of the problem? Are we cursed by God with disease, poverty, loneliness or "whatever" and to be plain, "just for being who we are"? Is that the underlying issue? How can I ever accept so great a gift as the Grace of God and his eternal salvation? Who do I thank?

John the Baptist expected Jesus to act in a certain way to protect him and free him from prison, but that was not God's plan. John was disappointed to hear the report of his disciples that Jesus would not be coming. John had no one to thank at that time. First Thessalonians tells us, "Rejoice always. Pray without ceasing; give thanks in ALL circumstances for this is the will of God in Christ Jesus for you.Do not quench the Spirit."1 Thess 5:15-19

How could John thank Jesus for "Not coming"? In his situation, he would likely be like many of us, questioning God and pleading,"Why me, God?". The lepers were healed. Of course they would thank God. But, First Thessalonians says I should be thankful in ALL circumstances, even the ones that appear doomed to failure. At he very least, when I am thankful in all circumstances, I am more likely to have a positive attitude. John knew he was going to be with Jesus in Heaven, regardless of his circumstances at that time. He could well have been thankful for that. Many at the time did not have such a hope.

I want to live with thankfulness on my lips, everyday!. When I thank the Giver, then, I believe, I am more likely to receive again. I believe it is not only good manners to thank the Giver of gifts, divine or otherwise. It is a foundational spiritual principle to believe that I have to "Top off my tank" with thanks before I can properly use what has been given. Then, as I use it and share with others, I will be ready to "fill up the tank again." We'll look at some very amazing physical gifts from "The Master" and what we might do with them in the next Chapter.

Like Eating Jelly With Chop Sticks　　　　　　　　　　　　　　　　　　Jack Narvel

Chapter 4

The Parable of the Ten Minas - How Should I Use My Gifts?

In the Bible, most Christians are familiar with the story of "The Ten Minas," as told in the Book of Luke (Luke 19:11-27) There is another Bible story in Matthew known as "The Parable of the Talents," (Matt 25:14-30). In both cases, the Word is telling us about "Gifts." Both stories have to do with money and financial stewardship. In Matthew, the rich man gives each of his servants "Five Talents." In Luke the master gives each of his servants "One Mina."

In both passages, I always thought the amount given to each man was small. Then, I was surprised to see the richness of the rewards they were given when their master returned. Looking up the value of these coins, as I had never done before writing this book, I was surprised that according to www.biblegateway.com, "A 'Talent' was equal to about twenty years of a day laborer's wage." In Luke they are given "One Mina." According to www.biblegateway.com the Mina was worth about "three months wages" for a day laborer. In these two stories, there is huge difference in the investment the master made in his servants. Yet, the stories Jesus told were not to illustrate the amount of the gift/investment but to illustrate what different people do with the same "gift," and how the "Master" (God) rewards them. Let's look at Luke here.

Luke was writing about a denomination of money, which in his day, had a value greater than a "mite" and greater than a Shekel, but not "incredible value." The Mina was a coin with the value of about fifty Shekels of silver. In U.S. dollars today, it would be about $2,160.00. The "Talent" was worth far more. We'll look at that in more detail later.

Here's a recap of Luke's story: A "nobleman" went on a journey and entrusted his ten servants with some money. Each of the ten was given one Mina. The nobleman said to them, "Engage in business until I come." (Luke19:11-27.ESV) It is unclear from the text what specific expectations the nobleman had of his servants as they, "engaged in business."

We do know from that story, when the owner returned, only three servants of the ten are mentioned. One servant had turned the one mina into ten, another turned it into five and another confessed he had simply hidden the coin without "engaging in business."

In Luke's story, the nobleman rewards those who brought him profit by giving them authority over cities in his new Kingdom. The one, who returned the nobleman's investment ten times, was given ten cities, the one who returned five times the investment was given five cities and the one who had hidden the coin had the coin taken away from him and given to the one who already had ten Minas.

It has occurred to me to ask, "Were the ten Minas 'gifts' to his servants, or were the coins seen as 'investments' with the expectation of profit? Were these people seen as his 'business partners', rather than his servants?"

If the latter were the case, then, inferring a message to us from this story, what are God's expectations of the gifts he gives us? Are they like birthday presents, seen by God as a gesture of love, with no expectation of return, or is God more like the nobleman who gives something of value to his servants, expecting that He will experience a return of value to His Kingdom?

The Bible talks about fruit coming from the branches. We are connected to God as we believe in Him and receive from Him. In the book of John, Jesus states," I am the Vine; you are the branches. Whoever abides in Me and I in him, he it is that bears much fruit. Apart from Me, you can do nothing." (John 15:5.ESV)

What is the value of a "gift" of any kind? Will we be given "Minas" or "Talents"? The Bible stories remind us that the amount we are given is not as important as how we use it in God's Kingdom.

God gives us gifts, and so do people. Gift giving is a time-honored tradition in our culture. We do it at birthdays and Christmas, as in the story in Chapter Two. But if God's gifts to us are not "gifts" but "investments" in His Kingdom, then maybe we will have to "work hard" for God in order to repay His gift of salvation? After all, He died a horrible death to "excuse our crimes." Should we not, in return, serve a "life sentence of humbling or even 'demeaning' works" to repay Him?

We often misconstrue the Bible's teachings to fit a set of beliefs which are not Biblical. Work is indeed commanded for Christians. In the book of James, we find," for just as the body without the spirit is dead, so also faith without works is dead." (James 2:26 NASB). But our works **should be** a byproduct of the Grace we have been given. We do not "earn our gifts" by "working for God." If we did, then they would not be "gifts," they would be "wages" or "rewards."

The Bible **does tell us** that there are "rewards" for believers in Heaven. See more about that in Chapter 6. But for now, let me simply say that the rewards we receive in Heaven will glorify God more than ourselves. But those rewards **will** provide us with joy as we recall the works that God did with us and through us and in us, while we were on earth.

Too many people reverse those two things. The idea of "earning salvation" is actually a tenant of Buddhism, where we reach "Heaven" (Nirvana) by appropriately following the tasks laid out in the "eightfold path." The truth is that all "religions of the world"(except Christianity) rely on the appropriate exercise of works to please God.

If you can't obey all of the 613 Command of the Law of Moses, then at least, as in Eastern Religions, you should leave the world a better place when you die, than the one you inherited. Law and grace should not be mixed as a salvation cocktail. We were not intended by God for "our works being applied to justify our salvation." These are misappropriations of the Gospel. Let's examine the exercise of gifts in a different context.

Have you ever had a friend or a co-worker, a boyfriend or a girlfriend who gave you such an unexpected and lavish gift that, instead of saying: "Wow, thanks so very much!," you said, "I'm sorry I can't possibly accept this gift." The giver may be shocked and ask: "Why not?"

The actual reason may be stuck in a myriad of past memories. You may feel that in the past you have not given **them** enough. You may feel that you must "trade favors" rather than simply accepting a favor and not worry about reciprocating. The key to this verbal transaction between giver and receiver may come back to our perception of what "giving and receiving" mean.

Adam Grant has written a great book called <u>Give and Take - Why Helping Others Drives Our Success</u>. In his book, Grant says that he has found that some businessmen are driven by selfish motives, others are driven by charitable motives, others feel that "trading favors" is the best way to achieve "success." In Grant's book, he says that his research into business has led him to conclude that a practice of giving and thankfulness is <u>actually beneficial to a business as well as in personal relationships.</u>

Grant is not only a University of Pennsylvania, Wharton School, Professor of Economics but a magician. If you are reading this book online, you can go to, [https://www.youtube.com/watch?v=1baNQmnRCVw] to see Adam's amazing "Rabbit Trail" on giving and receiving.

Getting back to God's giving and our receiving, God is the ultimate "gift giver." The Lord knows us very well. He will always give appropriate gifts. The enemy of our souls seeks to steal His gifts from us and even destroy us, or at least our testimony. The enemy seeks to convince us that we are unworthy; or like Adam and Eve that we are not already "like God" (created in His image) and that we "must do something" to earn or receive what is already ours. It is the enemy's strategy to always make us doubt who we are. He will try to make us doubt the value of what we already have. As he did with Adam and Eve he will seek to neutralize our faith through his instilled "self-doubt".

Since Adam and Eve, the problem we have as human beings is feeling unworthy to receive **any** gifts. Gifts, expensive ones or inexpensive ones, make little difference if we feel unworthy. We have a "gift giving Daddy" who loves to treat us lavishly. But we must feel worthy to receive the blessings he has for us.

Otherwise we may feel <u>even less</u> self worth. Ironic isn't it. We feel less self worth when we receive valuable gifts because they remind us how "unworthy" we are. Oh my goodness!

Is there a limit to God's blessing for us? Will He give children to a barren wife? Will He restore health to a person diagnosed with terminal cancer? Will He allow Million Dollar Lottery winnings to be given to a faithful believer?

Some believers think that buying Lotto tickets is a sin. But it may be Biblical. Why just look at Proverbs," The Lot is cast into the lap, but it's every decision is from The Lord."(Proverbs 16:33 ESV). It seems the best translation of the verse, to my mind, is the CEV: "We make our own decisions, but the Lord alone determines what happens."(Proverbs 16:33 CEV)

These verses, of course are not about how God may reward us for investing money in stocks or Lotto tickets, it's about how we are to know what God's will is for our lives and perhaps his possible intervention. More about this in Chapter 5.

God used my mother to give me the biggest stuffed elephant I had ever seen. I would have loved to have given Santa a big hug if I could have found him. I thought he was the one who gave the gift to me. There is a proper state of mind in which we can successfully receive, without guilt. Who really should I thank? Do I write an appropriate thank you card to someone? Do I even really need to be thankful?

The Bible states clearly that thanking God is an appropriate response to all God has given us. Also, "praising Him" may also be a good idea.

We are to pray, or converse with the Lord, about all things in our lives."Continue steadfastly in prayer, being watchful in it with thanksgiving."(Colossians 4:2 ESV). We need to watch our attitudes in prayer, that we are not begging God for a specific outcome, but rather conversing with Him about his best for us and for His Kingdom. After all, if you think about it, what King (good or bad) would wish to destroy his kingdom? So trust in God for the outcome and thank Him for what He is doing, however difficult it may be to see Him in it. Remember, The opposite of thankfulness is not "un-thankfulness," but "complaining"!

Let's get back to the stories of the Minas and the Talents. If God gave us five Talents, today, the value of a day laborer's work at fifteen dollars per hour, eight hours a day, six days a week, for twenty years, multiplied by five, then the value of the five Talents would have been $3,744,000.00. Please do the math yourself, I may be wrong.

The value of the one Mina would come in at $2,160.00. You can easily see that the doubling of the five Talents might have been worth the cost of ten small cities. On the other hand the value of the Mina, ten times, would have only been $21,000.00. Hardly the value of even one "whistle stop town" today.

But the point of both stories is not how much the servants were given to start with, nor the end result of how they were blessed The point is that God rewards our faithfulness with what He has given us, whether it's a few Hundred dollars or a Million Dollars; whether it's wages or a prize. It IS all from Him. God generously rewards his children for their faithfulness, whether a little or a lot. Here's the promise of God,"Bring all the tithes (ten percent of your gross income) into the storehouse, that there may be food in My house, and try me now in this, says the Lord of Hosts, if I will not open for you the windows of Heaven and pour out for you such blessings that there will not be room enough to receive it. AND I will rebuke the devourer for your sakes, so that he will not destroy the fruit of your ground"(Malachi 3:10-11 NKJV).

If you ponder this saying, you must come to the conclusion that God will multiply back to you, generously, whatever you give! The "ten percent" seed you have given Him as an offering in Church will grow. "But," you may say,"what if my experience is that I have given faithfully for many years? I have to admit, we have never gone to bed hungry nor woken up homeless. However, I could not say we have been 'blessed beyond measure.' Are we doing something wrong?" There may be a misunderstanding.

God will not necessarily give you the Million Dollar Lottery Ticket, just because you have faithfully given in Church. In fact the one who gets that winning ticket might not even be a believer. Stuff Happens! Do I turn to unbelief because my expectations are not met? No!

Longing for different circumstances can lead to complaining, and even a form of relationship damaging self-centeredness. The Israelites were familiar with this dilemma. It seems they were never satisfied and always griping about God's provision. We see the story in Exodus 16, God's people complained about the lack of tasty food such as they had in Egypt at slaves. So God provided for His people in the wilderness by sending them quail and "Manna." Yet, by Exodus 1, we are told they began craving other food and water, instead trusting God and rejoicing over what they had been given. Their complaints did not go down well with Moses or God at that time. Complaining never goes down well. Not with God, not with your family, your neighbors nor your co-workers today.

God DID send water from a Rock and abundance of manna to eat for forty years while they were in the desert. The manna was to be eaten every day while it was fresh in the mornings. Only on Saturdays was there no new manna, but Moses instructed them to gather twice as much on Friday and store half overnight for the Sabbath. If they tried to hoard manna overnight on any other day, it would rot.

When we try to "store up," or hoard abundance or immediately consume an overwhelming blessing, it seldom works out well. Think of the sudden "Lottery Winner Millionaires" who say they will give money to the Church, or even build a Church. Then, despite good intentions, the use of their sudden wealth sometimes turns out very badly. If you wish to take the time to read a sad story of such a Lotto winner, this Washington Post article tells it all. You can get the gist of it just in the headline:
https://www.washingtonpost.com/history/2018/10/24/jack-whittaker-powerball-lottery-winners-life-was-ruined-after-m-jackpot/

Quick riches are seldom the answer to life's issues. So instead of griping, why not be like King David. David is usually clearly singing praises to God and thanking Him for His creation of David and his Kingdom. Always a good idea to complete any transaction with another, whether God or man, by thanks.

Aside from money or manna, God gives us the free gift of His undeserved Grace and Mercy, because He loves us. In Romans, we see the correct attitude we should have toward God's gifts."You surely don't think much of God's wonderful goodness of His patience and willingness to put up with you.

Don't you know that the reason that God is good to you is because He wants you to turn to Him." (Romans 2:4 CEV)

When we engage in "tithing," or making "offerings" to charitable causes; it's not about the amount of the "return on your investment." God is different than the Stock Market or a Bond Fund. He gives generously as we are willing to receive it, and as we are thankful to Him for the gift, whatever its size. We should not be trying to "pay God back" for the sacrifice He made for us. We should not be doing "divine bookkeeping" regarding the return on our gifts. Rather, we should be thankful for all that we have and be ready to receive even more, **regardless** of the amount of the return or our circumstances. It's also a "Godly idea" to "pay forward" to others His generosity toward us. Again, regardless of the amount.

Like Eating Jelly With Chop Sticks　　　　　　　　　　　　　　　　　　Jack Narvel

Like Eating Jelly With Chop Sticks   Jack Narvel

Chapter 5

The Restaurant Owner is Looking Out for You

As I look back over my 74 years of life, I can find at least four instances where my life was spared, or at least serious injury was avoided. But to what purpose? Why would God preserve my life, or prevent me from incurring serious injury? I would have asked that question several times during my life if I had been of a clear enough mindset to even formulate it.

Each year in America, as we look back on the attacks and destruction of "9/11," many recall how the "miracles of a missed bus" or the delay taken to receive a phone call kept people from being killed in their offices that day.

I was reminded of these incidents recently when on the evening of July 19th, 2018 a "Duck-Boat" went down at Table Rock Lake, near Branson, Missouri. There appeared to be a sudden thunderstorm causing 5-foot waves to occur on this usually placid reservoir. The waves overwhelmed the low riding boat, causing the boat's engine to stall and the boat to quickly sink.

A woman lost three of her children and 6 other family members that day. In all, seventeen people, including the boat Captain, lost their lives in this accident. The woman's family had traveled from Indiana to gather for a "fun family reunion" in Branson. After all, was said and done and the wreckage of the boat recovered, the woman and her thirteen-year-old nephew were the only survivors of her immediate family. As we read about incidences such as this, we have to ask ourselves why God appears to spare some and not others? This is a profound question that has been asked by both believers and unbelievers over the Centuries.

The tie in for me, with my own story of God's Grace, in sparing my life, was the mother's statement that she was praying as the boat was sinking that God would "save her children." When the children were later found deceased, I believe that this event would have caused a great deal of heartache, not only for her, but in <u>any believer or unbeliever</u>, under similar circumstances. Like John the Baptist in the King's Dungeon, she must have been asking,"Lord, Why me?"

We pray to God; we trust in Him to guide and lead us, and yes, we even count on Him to save us from physical danger. If He is really "all-powerful," "all present" and oh, by the way: "God is in control," how can these things happen?. Well, to some, the death or injury of "unbelievers," may be expected as part of "the wrath of God," as detailed in many Old Testament stories. We are given in our "Religious, Church upbringing" that "the wages of sin are death," applies, still today, to believers and unbelievers alike.

I remember reading a Religious Pamphlet about the onset of Cancer. The title was "The Curse Causeless Will Not Come." The text clearly stated that it was our own sin which caused the onset of serious illness or death. (Job's comforters must have written that pamphlet.) As those friends of Job told him, he should have kept his life on "the straight and narrow path." Job's tragedies were of his own making, according to his "comforters," as are ours today! God will take his terrible vengeance on us for any "slips,""errors," or (God forbid) SIN! This is what "Religion" teaches us.

Like Eating Jelly With Chop Sticks — Jack Narvel

"So there! and You deserved it!" Like Job's "comforters," the "The Religious among us" often look for, and speak of, a cause and effect relationship between our actions and God's response. It is as though "The Church" believes that we are able to control directly the actions of an almighty and all powerful God. Talk about "Putting God in a Box!" According to The Law of Moses, we could expect blessings from God when we obeyed His Commandments and curses when we disobeyed. God put Himself in that "box" as part of the covenant agreement he made with the Israelites. He is <u>no longer in that box</u> for us as believers.

In "Religion" God is a figure of terror to both the unbeliever and the believer! Once "saved" we could count on His love never to depart from us. But His wrath MIGHT still apply, if we didn't "behave ourselves." Today, as adults, we see that "sinners and crooks" may prevail, at least for a while. We see the innocent, even believers, such as the family in Branson, die. It's "just not fair" is it?

God says in His New Covenant that it is" not His wish for any to perish, but for all to come to repentance."(2nd Peter 3:9 NET) Of course, that statement is not about physical life or death. It's about eternal life with God. So our question, and Job's question, is why are so many people sick, dying, or being killed in accidents? Is it a "False Gospel" to believe that "God is always in control?"

Have you ever heard anyone say that the reason a good family member died at a young age was because "God needed them to be with Him in Heaven, so He called them home." This is hardly a statement of "condolence" that brings one comfort.

Rather it may inspire "anger at God." I've seen many cases where that was true.

Aside from simply believing and trusting Him what must we do? What is our part in this amazing drama of life with God? If "God is Love" does love, by definition, always give us a choice? Or, instead, is God "always in control," like a benign dictator?

Let's examine that philosophy of "God as dictator," versus "God as a loving father" who wishes the best for us. Let's look at ourselves as a literal "child" of God for a moment.

God is our Daddy, Jesus is our brother and the Holy Spirit lives in us (if we believe that Jesus died for our sin and was resurrected to live and intercede for us at His throne at the right hand of Father God). As Earthly children, we believe that "Daddy knows everything" (at least until we find out he doesn't, around age nine or ten, at the latest). My nephew once asked his mother a question she couldn't answer. She said,"I don't know, Honey." His response was,"Well, Google it, Mommy!" Mommies may not know, but Daddies and Google always do!

We are told to believe that if we listen to Daddy he will steer us in the right direction and prevent harm from coming to us. If daddy is an abusive drunk, we may quickly learn that he cannot be trusted. If he's "normal" we may turn about nine or ten, at the latest, before we stop "believing completely in Daddy." Our Heavenly Daddy should be different. The Apostle Paul writes in Romans that "Christ sits at the right hand of God, pleading for us. Can anything ever separate us from Christ's love?" (Romans 8:34-38 NLT)

If what Paul writes in Romans is so, then God must no longer love us if we have trouble or calamity. Are we separated from

God's love in a calamity? Or, perhaps it's just me, then. I get caught up in the events of the day and retreat, separating myself from God. The Apostle Paul writes,"No, but I am convinced that nothing can ever separate us from God's Love. Neither death nor life, neither angels nor demons, neither our fears for today nor our worries about tomorrow - not even the powers of hell can separate us from God's love." (Rom8:38.NLT). By this passage, <u>even I</u> (in my rebellious and hateful attitudes) <u>cannot separate myself from God.</u> Could that really be true?

The lesson here for me is that whether I am sick or well, even dead or alive, God is still loving me. Once united with Him, through my acceptance of Jesus as my Lord and Savior, I can never be separated from Him again.

If my loving Father would give me some advice, which might even cause my life on this earth to be spared, I would take it… right? But is my Heavenly Father like my Earthly father? Does his advice sometimes fail? Does He "beat me with His divine belt" when I go against His advice? Does He sometimes "look the other way" and ignore us? Or maybe we can't always trust His advice. How do we know the advice is from Him, anyway?

Theologians tell us that we can "hear" three voices talking to us in our heads. The voice might be God's, it might be our own voice, or it might be the enemy. We have to discern, through practice, which voice it is. As a result of imperfect listening, we don't always follow God's advice, do we? We often follow our own, even attributing our own desires to God. We might think we have followed God's leading, but often we don't even ask for it.

How do we get ourselves in trouble in the first place? If God is "always in control," then anything that happens, which is, at least in our minds, "bad," would be "all God's fault." Not only the death of the family in the Duck Boat accident, but how about over six million Jews killed by the Nazis in World War Two? Is that really "all on God"? Or, were there choices being made, not just in Germany, but in other countries which contributed to that end result?

We learn from history that Adolf Hitler wanted to be rid of the Jews. Initially he did not want to kill them, just expel them and steal their property. He allowed the S.S. St Louis with 937 Jewish Refugees on board to sail for Cuba. Only 28 were permitted to disembark. The U.S. and Canada both refused to accept the Jewish refugees and the St. Louis was returned to Europe. The choices other countries were making at that time may have convinced Hitler that he was right to deal with the Jews in any way he saw fit, which would include taking their valuables, enslaving them, imprisoning them and, of course, exterminating them in "Death Camps" throughout Europe.

If God was in charge at that time, there were certainly a lot of people who weren't "buckling under His rule." We must ask ourselves, "How do our choices affect us personally, beyond today and how do our choices affect others?"

So that covers my responsibility when "bad stuff happens". That can't be on me. On the other hand, when "good things happen" it is probably because something I have done has pleased God beyond measure and I am being rewarded. How can we behave to be sure?

We are told in the Bible that it is the enemy's "Modus Operandi" (M.O.) to "steal, kill and destroy." We live in a "Fallen

World" as the result of Adam and Eve's sin against God in the Garden of Eden. According to Genesis 1:26, God created all things on Earth, then He gave mankind dominion over all things on Earth. In Genesis 2, God creates Eve as a "helper" for Adam. Eve ends up "helping" Adam to believe the lies of the enemy. But… Adam made the final choice, didn't he?

Besides killing and destroying, we are told that the enemy often "twists the truth" to suit his own purposes. As a result of this tendency on the enemy's part Adam and Eve were both led astray. The enemy told them that if they would eat of the tree of "The Knowledge of Good and Evil," they would be "like God." They point they missed, and that we often miss today, is that we are already "like God." We are all created in His image. Oops!

Adam and Eve violated the only command they had ever been given: "Don't eat the fruit from the tree of the knowledge of good and evil" After breaking this one and only law, they were subsequently banished from the Garden, so they would not be able to eat from "the Tree of Life" and live eternally, "like God."

Many would say that banishment from the Garden was God's punishment for their disobedience. Others would say God banished them after tasting the fruit of the tree of The Knowledge of Good and Evil, to protect them from an eternal life of "self-judgment" constantly weighing their behavior, and the behaviors of others, against a standard of "Good" or "Evil."

Apparently, banishment from the Garden did not stop us from judging ourselves and others, by a "standard impossible to uphold." We still make choices based on incomplete information and then suffer the consequences. God **could** have prevented our actions and thus the consequences, but His gift of "free will' to us prohibits His interference in most situations.

I said earlier that the Branson Duck Boat story (which ran in the papers and on television in July of 2018) reminded me of four events in my own life where the choices I'd made, or the circumstances surrounding them, could have had serious consequences, even death. And yet my life was spared. Here they are in order of my life's timeline.

1). The first was my enlistment in the Army in November of 1968. The Vietnam War was was already on. I had met "the love of my life" and we intended to marry in December. I had hoped to be exempted from Service. but the exemption from Service for married couples had recently been removed. My wife suggested we move to Canada to avoid my being sent to Vietnam, but I had concerns!

I did not speak Canadian and was not aware of any job openings there. I had no friends who were Canadian and I did not subscribe to the "Toronto Sun." "LinkedIn" was not yet on the internet to allow me to search for Canadian jobs. In fact, in 1968, there wasn't much on the Internet at all. I'm not even sure Al Gore had invented the internet at that time.

Since I was unable to find a place to work and live in Canada, I convinced my wife I would be better off talking to my Uncle Ed Greenwood who was chairman of the local Draft Board. I asked Uncle Ed if I could be a "conscientious objector" to avoid active duty in a "war zone"? After all, I had never shot anything, other than a crow.

About that crow, while visiting friends who owned a farm, I was loaned a 22 over 410 rifle. I saw a crow on the roof of their barn and figured I should try out the rifle. I aimed and shot the bird with one try. It was about a 75 yard shot. At first, I was proud I hit the bird. But then, I felt awful, as the bird plummeted from the roof of their barn. It was D.O.A. in the driveway! My one shot had gone directly through the side of his head. I put the rife away and never wanted to shoot anything ever again. Despite my telling Ed this story, he affirmed, "You can't qualify as a conscientious objector with your set of beliefs." Hmmm. Well, I'd affirmed I didn't wish to be involved in killing anything or anyone. Wouldn't that be enough? Apparently not.

According to Uncle Ed (an attorney) the laws regarding Military Service clearly stated that the "set of beliefs" which would permit me to become a "conscientious objector" would have to involve God's direction of my life in some way. Instead, my plea to be recognized as a C.O. was the result of my own "fleshly" desire not to be put "in harm's way"

I knew I was losing the argument, and Ed was a practicing attorney, so I asked him "What would you advise me to do?" His immediate response was," Do the same thing I told my own son to do: 'Enlist!'" Of course, Ed's son was a medical doctor who just needed a residency to complete his degree. When my cousin Richard enlisted, his assignment was to work and finish his degree at the Naval Hospital in Pensacola, Florida. Yes, Pensacola could be hot and stormy, but it WAS arguably safer than an assignment in Vietnam.

Now, I had to go back to Dana, and tell her my Uncle's advice. He had suggested I go to the recruiter and sign up for the delayed enlistment Officer Candidate School (OCS) program. That way, as an officer, I might have a better chance of avoiding combat and having an assignment elsewhere than Vietnam. I would also be able to get an "early drop" from my service in order to return and complete my Master's Degree at Penn. And, who knew, by the time I finished eight weeks of Basic Training at

Ft. Dix, New Jersey, eight weeks of AIT (Advanced Infantry Training) elsewhere and then twelve weeks of OCS, at Ft. Benning, Georgia, the war might even be over! Hooray!

Dana wasn't buying it. She still thought Canada was the best choice. However, I had no desire to become a felon, convicted of deserting his country in time of War. My Uncle Ed would doubtless have prosecuted my case! Ah, families.

Against my her better advice, I went to the Selective Service Center in Philadelphia for a medical exam. Perhaps I could be deferred into a non-combative role by my lack of "physical preparedness!" In the Second Millenia, there are minimum physical standards a "recruit" must meet. That was NOT true in the 1960s. Any shape or size was welcome.

During my exam, I directed the doctors to my poor eyesight (20/600 in my left eye, 20/200 in my right). The doctor assured me that the prescription eyeglasses, with which the Army would provide me, would not only correct my vision to 20/20 but that "the newer plastic lenses would resist scratching and serve me well in any combat situation." You may imagine how much better that pronouncement made me feel about serving. If I got free glasses that corrected my vision to 20/20, that would surely make up for my risking my life. That the glasses would not break or shatter if I came under fire, was another "plus."

Next, I mentioned to the examining physician my "Chronic Sinusitis." I had trouble breathing sometimes and I had issues with pollen. The doctor asked me if I was a smoker. I said I was. He said, "give up smoking and sinusitis should no longer be a problem." I was not getting anywhere, even the fact that many of my muscles exhibited a flaccidity from disuse, would also be quickly corrected by the Army's renowned "weight loss and physical fitness program."

On that note, in the Fall of 1968, I went off to Fort Dix, New Jersey, instead of finishing my last year of Graduate School. My adventure in the Army began.

My close friend Jim, had preceded me into the military with similar goals of combat avoidance. He advised me to stick with the OCS program as long as I could stomach it, then drop out to check with Personnel. With the Personnel staff I could investigate what non-combatant options might be open. That's the path Jim took. He had ended up as a mechanic in the Army Motor Pool in Berlin, Germany. He had no skills in vehicle maintenance, of which I was aware. The Army must have taught Jim everything he needed to know to repair and maintain vehicles. The military is quite good at doing that. So with that hope of reassignment to a non combative role, off I went.

Having survived unscathed through my Basic Training at Fort Dix, I recall some defining moments of rifle marksmanship training. The temps were in the low single digits. The Range Officer said, "Just THINK about pulling the trigger of your M-14/A-1 Rifle, you don't even have to feel it." I was reminded of the musical movie,"The Music Man," where Professor Harold Hill assured his students that they could learn to play an instrument purely by using "The Think Method." It was so cold in December on the rifle range, my hands and fingers were numb. I could not feel anything, so I found that my instructors spoke accurately. I qualified as a "Marksman", through the use of "The Think Method"

Next, I was off to Ft Jackson South Carolina after a brief leave for Christmas, my wedding service and honeymoon in New

York. It is interesting to me, that while I was stationed at Ft. Jackson, I never knew that Myrtle Beach, South Carolina was only two hours away from it. Ironically later in life, God assigned me to Myrtle Beach.

I was getting used to the warmer weather that The South provided and was happy to be assigned to Ft. Benning, Georgia for OCS. But not knowing how completely I was enjoying Ft. Benning, my mother did her best to get me reassigned, without my knowledge.

It seems she wrote a letter to General William Westmoreland to plead the case that I was surely too smart and accomplished in the area of communications to be left as a foot soldier, or in command of foot soldiers. What a great Mom - always looking out for me, just like God, sort of.

One day, while training in OCS, I was called out of the field to the Colonel's office. There I heard for the first time about my mother's letter. She had read a magazine article in which General Westmoreland had stated that "Todays Army" was no longer throwing young men willy-nilly into the fray, but was "selecting and using individuals who had specific skills for specific areas of need." In light of that article, it was logical for my Mom to write General Westmoreland a letter telling him of her son's skills and how he might better serve the Army as a communications specialist.

Thus, the Colonel, responding to a direct order from General Westmoreland himself, asked if I would care to be re-assigned to the Signal Corps? He said, if so, I would be re-assigned to Fort Belvoir, Maryland, to learn more about signals.

I innocently asked the Colonel what to expect after the additional training. Would I be assigned to a duty station **other** than Vietnam? He replied that Vietnam had the greatest demand of personnel of all skills at that time, Thus being in the Signal Corps would not keep me from assignment to a combat zone.

I thanked the Colonel for his time and excused myself saying, I thought I would take my chances with the OCS training and see where that led.

Lest you think I was stupid to avoid the re-assignment, remember I was still looking forward to my planed visit with Personnel, after I dropped out of OCS. They would surely find an assignment that would keep me from "Harm's Way."

Thank God for Moms, even when we don't follow their advice, however well intentioned. The story of my Mom's letter to the General became a great and humorous tale for some years. The lesson to be learned from my mother's letter and its result, was that people in authority will often act to your benefit, when you call out their words and deeds against them. It could also have been that my Uncle Edward was more important than I had thought.

Back in training, I studied the rules of the Uniform Code of Military Justice, so that I might protect myself legally from any attacker of any rank. I was not aware of how handy this study might be until later in my training.

The UCMJ was unique in that it applied only to military personnel. It would have no standing in a civil court of law. So while I was in the military I would be subject to a code of law which had not applied to me as a civilian, and would not apply to me again, once I had left the service. Interesting. It was almost like living in two worlds at the same time. Similar, to some degree, to being a born-again Christian. A different set of Laws apply to me, as a believer… but more on that later.

In OCS, we had a marathon of classes, exercise, and "Study Hall" in the evenings. One evening, when all good Candidates should have been in their rooms studying the lessons of the day, I was instead writing a letter to my wife Dana, about how much I loved her and missed her. I was waxing very romantic, in a way that was laughable to anyone but she and I. My room was suddenly invaded by the Lieutenant in charge of another company on the floor below us. He had stopped in to check on all of us.

I don't know who gave him the authority to do that, since we were not under his direct command. None-the-less, he found my letter and read it chuckling to himself. He said, "Narvel, you know you are not allowed to write personal correspondence during study hall. You are disobeying a direct order." In the Bible this behavior of mine would be characterized as "transgression," the intentional violation of a law. But we were not under Biblical Law, we were under the Uniform Code of Military Justice. My behavior was also a violation of the UCMJ, violation of a direct order!

I think the Lieutenant was jealous! He took the letter off of my desk and said he was going downstairs to read it to his men, so they could enjoy his humor at my expense. I reminded him that under the UCMJ, he was not allowed to remove any personal property from my room without my direct permission. He laughed and dared me to do anything about it. Apparently, he had not bothered to read the UCMJ as it applied to OCS candidates and their superiors.

The next day, I made an appointment to see the Base Chaplain regarding "a concern." When I went to the Chaplain I told him the sordid details of the Lieutenant's foray into my room and his illegal transfer of my letter to his men on the floor below us.

I shared with the Chaplain that I heard the Lieutenant had read my letter to his entire platoon and they had laughed uproariously with him. When I confided those details with the Chaplain and cited the UCMJ code which had been violated, he promised to "take care of it."

A week later,I was told that the officer in question had been transferred to his new duty station in Vietnam. Truly it is said in Romans, "Dear friends, never take revenge. Leave that to the righteous anger of God. For the Scriptures say 'I will take revenge. I will pay them back', says The Lord."(Romans 12:19 NLT)

As I may have said before, I was not really walking with the Lord at this time in my life. Aside from my conversion, in fear of God's wrath on me, personally, when I was 13, I really had no "capital with God" to draw on at this point in my life. As my Uncle Ed had rightly discerned, I was not walking a path guided by the Holy Spirit, but my own Earthly desires to avoid personal harm.

After my incident with the Lieutenant, none of the other officers bothered to enforce punishments for any "wrongs" I had committed. I remember one officer asking me to "get down and give me 100 push-ups!" I started laughing as I was counting them out, "one sir, haha, two sir, giggle…" After about ten the officer said, "I give up, on you, Narvel," and walked away.

The moral of this story is that when you violate a law, such as "no personal correspondence during study hall," it is good to always be ready to defend yourself with another law!

The conclusion of this story ends in Vietnam where I once again met the officer who had read my personal mail to his men. We were delighted to see each other! He greeted me with a warm handshake and a hug. I was glad to see him alive and well. We caught up on personal details and I never saw him again. I assume he survived his tour as he was about ready to go home when we met. No hard feelings! God **is** good!

My "Life Saving" Personnel Department assignment was to train to be a Scout Dog Handler. In a Guerrilla War, you never knew where the enemy was. But a dog could sniff our their presence and alert the troops. The benefit to me was that I would spend 3 months training my dog "on leash" then the top 12 in the class (which would surely include me) would go on for another 2 months training "off leash". The top graduate of that class, (who would be me) would be held back at Ft. Benning to train other Dog Handlers.

As it turned out, I WAS the top graduate. Unfortunately, they had enough trainers already so the Army sent my dog and I off to the Combat Zone I had worked so hard to avoid. Dana again suggested we book passage to Canada and be done with the Army. But I hesitated to abandon my dog, with whom I had actually spent more time, than my wife Well, nearly….

Although there are a number of amusing tales during my time in Scout Dog Handler Training and deployment in Vietnam none were remotely life-threatening. As I read the bulletin board at the Fourth Division Base in Pleiku, listing current "Hot Spots," I was concerned; but in fact, I was never assigned to any of them, while they were "Hot."

One time, I was asked to take an assignment in Cambodia to go into a combat zone to discover and call-in support for the recovery bodies of downed pilots, who had parachuted out of their aircraft during the "Tet-Offensive." They had lost contact with their base and were expected to be in the woods in Cambodia, most likely dead.

This seemed like a "grisly," although possibly not a life-threatening assignment to me. I recalled that, our assignment as Scout Dog Handlers was to confirm enemy locations and to protect our troops while on patrol missions. Our duty assignment had nothing to do with finding bodies after their decease, rather keeping our troops from becoming such.

It seemed to me that this Cambodian assignment was clearly out of our direct responsibility. I tried to think of a way to escape this coming duty, short of deserting to Canada. As I pondered my dog's condition and my own, an excellent idea came to me to avoid this foray into Cambodia

Our Colonel was coming out to inspect the troops that evening, including both dogs and dog handlers. We were all decked out in our clean field uniforms. Our dogs were gathered in a sitting position (doggie version of "attention") at our side. In anticipation of this event, I managed to twist the truth to my advantage.

My dog Chris would get small cuts on his paws, like "paper cuts" from the gravel on the roads, which was sometimes sharp. I asked the Veterinary Technician for some gauze pads with which I dabbed and pressed my dog's paws. I then wrapped the pads, of both front feet, bloody side out, and stood at attention waiting for the Colonel. As he passed me by, he glanced at the dog's bloody feet, saying, "What's wrong with your dog's feet?" I replied, "Nothing Sir. He just gets these little 'paper cuts'; in his paws from the gravel in the road sometimes, Sir. But he's fine; he can work Sir!"

Upon my statement of this "Gung-Ho" and only slightly twisted truth, the Colonel said, "You keep that dog in for three days soldier, and have him checked by the Vet before you take him out again!" "Yes, Sir!" At your command, Sir!. And off I went with some other comrades to enjoy the bars and festive nightlife near our base in *Ban My Thuit.*

So if there it is. The story of my foray into Vietnam as a 11F2 Delta, Army Dog Handler. If there is, as yet, any doubt in your minds that I was playing life as safely as I could while in a war, please doubt no more!

I felt guilty about my "non-combatant-combatant role," when I moved to South Carolina, forty-three years after the Vietnam War. People in the South are very kind to the military and former military here. I felt I had not lived up to their kindness and respect.

After living in the Pacific Northwest, where people literally spat on soldiers, returning from service in Vietnam, at the Sea-Tac airport, it was quite a surprise to receive the respect which all military are given here.

I felt as though I didn't deserve that respect for the type of service I had given my country. Yes, I had gone out into the field with my dog on a weekly basis while in Vietnam, but I tried to find ways to go back to base without spending the maximum five days in the field that dogs were permitted. Infantrymen could stay out for a month without returning to Base, but dog took only five days, then they needed R&R. In my time in Vietnam, I was never in the line of enemy fire. I felt guilty that I had not done as much as others.

That guilt was dispelled when I got a call from the fiancee of one of my old dog detachment buddies, forty-eight years after we had left the service! His name is Jake and his dog's name was Missy. His fiancee called me after seeing my name and workplace on Facebook. She said that Jake still talked about me, even though we had not seen each other since we both returned to University following our discharge. She said she thought it would be good for Jake to re-connect with me.

I am not sure, to this day, what I had said or done with Jake to create such a lasting impression. But, after talking on the phone, we agreed to meet in Savannah, Georgia. Since he lived in Florida and I lived in South Carolina, that seemed like a great "middle ground." We got a hotel for both couples near downtown Savannah and had an excellent four days of getting reacquainted with each other and our ladies.

Near the end of our visit, I mentioned my feelings of guilt to Jake, regarding responding to folks saying, "Thank you for your service." He said, "Jack, our assignment as Scout Dog Handlers was to protect the men walking behind us in the field. In our time in Vietnam, none of the troops assigned to our covering was ever successfully attacked. No one was ever wounded or killed while with us. We did our jobs, Jack, and we did it well. You have no reason to feel anything but pride for your service in Vietnam." WOW!

Then I asked him why he remembered me so well through all those years. He said, "You were always a positive influence. You were always making even the most dire situations lighter. If I was worried about an upcoming assignment, you always had a way of making it seem like 'no big deal'. I always felt confidence and peace when you were with me." Hmmm

Was Jake's feeling of confidence and peace when I was with him a product of the fact that I had Christ living in me, even though I was mostly unaware of Him at the time?

As I have noted before, according to Romans, "For I am persuaded that neither death, nor life, nor angels nor principalities, nor powers nor things present, nor things to come. Nor height nor depth, nor any other creature, shall be able to separate us from the love of God, which is in Christ Jesus our Lord." (Romans 8:38-39 KJV)

In truth, I seldom was afraid when I was in Vietnam. Was the training I'd had at Ft. Benning, Ft. Jackson and Ft. Dix enough to have convinced me that I could rely on my fellow soldiers regardless of the situation? As I recall reliance on God was seldom, if ever, mentioned in our training.

We were in the middle of a "Guerrilla War," for Heaven's sake! A North Vietnam regular soldier, or sympathizer, could come around the corner and throw a grenade at you. A Viet Cong sympathizer could be cleaning your "Hootch"(barracks) and stab you in the back as you returned. A child begging for candy could be concealing a hand-grenade behind his back. There could be a Claymore Mine, with a tripwire detonator, set across the entry to the toilets. (which there was once). There was always an unknown level of threat, as soon as you crossed the border to Vietnam or Cambodia.

Aside from mental incapacity, my lack of fear in this time of war may have been due to the tendency, of even healthy men to compartmentalize our thinking. We tend to "push down" thoughts and emotions which appear to be counterproductive to our current situation The resulting "explosion" of these repressed thoughts and emotions, after the conflict is over and we are safely home, results in what psychologists call "PTSD" (Post Traumatic Stress Disorder.)

But the Word says, instead of falling prey to the temptation to analyze and categorize and "replay" the events typical of war; we should rather, allow the "Peace of God, which surpasses every understanding, (to) … guard your hearts and your thoughts by Christ Jesus."(Phil 4:7 WEB)

That "shalom peace" is promised to believers. It is a feeling of well being in body, soul, mind, and spirit.

"Don't worry about anything, instead pray about everything. Tell God what you need and thank Him for all He has done. Then you will experience God's peace, which exceeds anything we can understand. His peace will guard your hearts and minds as you live in Christ Jesus."(Phil 4:6-7 NLT)

That passage makes no sense to me when applied to my life in Vietnam. I was not "trusting in God" to protect me, yet I felt a sense of peace most of the time. I was not "thanking God" for all He had done in my life or was going to do. Yet I felt that peace. Does a relationship, like "Loving Father and Son" redefine all the thinking we may have done about God's character in the past? I believe it does. I certainly give Him credit for protecting me and the men I served within Vietnam. I am aware of many who gave their lives in Vietnam, for a cause which many thought was questionable. But I am only convinced that I had God's love with me and for me and my life was spared for that reason.

Unfortunately, my refusal to take my wife to Canada, resulted in my first divorce. Her opinion was that if I had "really loved her", I would never have left her. So after I finished Graduate School, I picked up my few belongings and moved to San Francisco to pursue life as a "Hippie". My Apartment had been cleaned out of its valuable items by a druggy hanger on who knew I would not have room in my Volkswagen Bug for everything I had in my apartment. He was very self sacrificing in taking everything and carrying it down three flights of stairs. It was "all good"

2) The second time God spared my life was after Vietnam when I returned to Philadelphia and the University of Pennsylvania to complete my interrupted Master's Degree. I met a guy named Jerry, through a mutual friend, who found out that I was teaching a photography class as part of my Master's Degree work. He wanted me to teach him about taking pictures, developing film and making prints. In return, he would introduce me to his girlfriends. We could take pictures of them after hours in the studios at the University. Jerry would develop and print and make points with his girlfriends.

Jerry and I created backdrops with slides to make the scenes more realistic. The resulting photos were black and white, to enable Jerry and I to enjoy the full experience of "the process of photography." Photography is not nearly as fun today, with instant digital results and the ability to edit photos on your cell phone. Ah, well…

One night, after some of our inspirational work at the University, Jerry suggested a ride on his Triumph 750 Tiger motorcycle. I had never been into Motorcycles or Sports Cars, but it was a warm summer night and …"Why Not?" We cruised down two-lane country roads outside Philadelphia for about two hours. I was definitely enjoying the wind in my long "Hippie" hair and the feel of the warm breeze on my skin. We returned to the city at about 1 A.M.

As we were sitting at a stoplight, another young man on his "hot rod" motorcycle pulled up next to us. He twisted his handgrips to make his motorcycle "rev." Jerry responded in kind, also "twisting and reviving." Soon the light changed and both drivers let out their clutches. As Jerry was not compensating for the extra weight on the back of his bike by leaning forward (and asking me to do the same), we quickly spun over backward. The right side of my head made smart contact with the curb of the sidewalk next to us.

Of course, we were brave men and had no need to wear helmets or other protective gear. Shortly after that, Jerry took me to the University of Pennsylvania Hospital. That medical facility was certainly "State of the Art" for the 1970s. There was no hospital finer on the East Coast, short of Johns Hopkins Medical Center.

The resident Physician on duty examined my wound. He said I might need some stitches to close the wound. I said,"Well, 'suture' self, Doc." He didn't laugh. I asked,"Heard that one before?" He nodded as he cleaned me up and told me, "You probably ought to have an X-Ray, but it's 2 A.M., and there are no more techs on duty. Please come back in the morning. Here's some Darvon for your pain."

Now, in the year 2019, people would have been fired for that recommendation. But I had experienced no unconsciousness, I had no signs of a concussion. For all intents and purposes, I had just experienced a cut on the side of my head from rubbing on an unforgiving piece of concrete. So Jerry took me home and I took a taxi back to the hospital in the morning.

The next day, the X-Ray techs were back in force. They examined my prints with shock and disbelief on their faces. I had a depressed skull fracture the size of a ping-pong ball. I was immediately admitted. The night staff was doubtless roundly scolded for sending me home. "You could have died in the night with that injury. Do you live with anyone who could have helped you?" No, Doc. no one.

I imagined loud shrieks reverberating inside the Doc's head as he imagined the lawsuits from my uncle and family, had I indeed died as the result of a bad decision at the U of P Hospital. Even though my mother, my uncle and grandfather had graduated from the U of P, I think they would have required appropriate retribution on the institution which had killed their relative through negligence.

I had surgery, stayed in the hospital for a week and was released with half of my head shaved and the other half with shoulder-length hair remaining. My first stop upon my release was to my barber. My barber always claimed to be good friends with several "Philly Mafiosa," but when my Volkswagen sedan was stolen and parted out (doubtless by organized crime), he said, "I'm sorry Doc, but I can't help you with that." So much for criminal friendships.

I had no after-effects of my injuries, except that I still have a six-inch-long mini canyon depression on the right side of my head. Again, I was certainly not experiencing the leading of the Holy Spirit, throughout all these events, but for some reason, I thought, there MUST be a reason my life was being preserved against all odds.

While living the "Hippie Life" in San Francisco, I became a musician part time and the Purchasing Manager for a start up electronics firm which made "Biofeedback" instruments. These instruments were briefly popular with the medical community in the early '70's until they realized that people could actually learn to control their "unconscious physiological responses", and probably wouldn't need as much medicine, or even the Doctor himself. God actually gave us authority over the functions of our own bodies in Genesis Chapter 1. But it was at this time, that I discovered that authority was real. Again - I wasn't consciously walking with God, but He kept teaching me valuable stuff, anyway. It was at this time, as a musician that I met and married my second wife, Diane. My marriage to Diane and our move from San Francisco to Chicago, leads me into my next story of God's Grace.

3) The third unlikely rescue occurred at Christmas in 1989, My wife and I were unable to have children by natural birth. After six years of trying artificial insemination and other means, we elected to adopt a family of three children, ages two, four and six. The next year we took the brother of the three, who had just been born in March. Then we had four children in foster care, pending legal adoption. But I get ahead of myself.

We were living in the Chicago suburb of Itasca, Illinois, at the time. We suddenly had three children in our house the week before Christmas. As you may imagine, it was a challenging and festive Christmas with four new young people to absorb into our family of two. Oh, and did I mention, we had also invited my wife's parents to join us in welcoming the children as we celebrated Christ's birth.

Some highlights of Christmas Day: were my oldest daughter, Hannah, pulling the Christmas tree down on Grandma, and the same daughter breaking my wife's favorite "collector jar" of perfume. Never having had a "proper Christmas with presents before," the children all slept in past eight A.M.

We had to wake them up and tell them that Santa had come and there were presents waiting for them downstairs. They had no idea. They got into the festivities briefly, but around Eleven A.M., my oldest, David, asked if they could go back to bed. "We're pretty tired, Daddy," he said. Can I hear anyone say. "Christmas! Bah, Humbug!" But back to the presents.

One of those presents were three "Turbo Tubes," made of inflatable thick and slick plastic with handles on two sides. There was a clear warning label in their package which said, "DO NOT USE NEAR TREES." The phrase was in BIG letters which any attentive parent could not miss. So on New Years eve of 1989, I took the three kids out to a local golf course, with a somewhat elevated third green, to try out their new sleds. It had just snowed and there was several inches of new snow, over the old (somewhat icy) snow.

The kids did great heading down the hill at reasonable speed and stopping well short of the tree line at the bottom of the hill. Did I mention the warning label that said,"Do not use near trees?" Oh yes, I did….

After these three successful runs, Daddy decided to follow the same run as the kids. Daddy was forgetting that he weighed three times as much as the kids and the laws of physics, particularly, that of "Inertia" might dictate that Daddy would go further than the kids.

To add extra fun to the sled run, there was a cart path about half way down the hill. As the kids hit it they bounced and laughed. As Daddy hit that same path, the Turbo Tube threw Daddy in the air. Daddy was suddenly upside down, looking up, rather than forward, and headed for the tree line!

Sensing what was coming, I folded my hands over my head to protect myself from what might have been a permanently incapacitating head injury. Sure enough, my premonition was correct. Moments later, the backs of my hands and wrist encountered the firm trunk of an Oak tree.

The kids immediately rallied to me and asked if Daddy was O.K.? "Yes, I'm fine, but I think we need to pick up our Turbo Tubes and go home."

I frankly didn't remember the drive home at the time; nor do I remember it today. It was about a six mile drive and the kids later said that I seemed to be driving the van, "a little crazy." I am still amazed, not only that I wasn't killed or permanently paralyzed by hitting the tree; I am also amazed that God protected us in our drive home, even as I was slipping in and out of consciousness.

When we got home, my son David, aged six, announced to my wife,"Mommy, Daddy had an accident.." "What happened?," she asked. After a somewhat garbled account about our sledding adventure proceeded from the mouths of both David and Hannah, I said," I think Daddy just needs a hot bath." My wife responded,"I think Daddy needs a hospital!"

Now recall, if you will, that it was New Years Eve, but unlike my motorcycle hospital experience, the emergency staff and X-Ray techs at Alexian Brothers Hospital were all on duty! It was still afternoon. As the X-Ray films were developed, it was determined that I had broken both bones of my right wrist and my C-5 was cracked. So the Docs gave me some Morphine and pulled my arm out to straighten and set the wrist bones. Even with the Morphine the sensation was, might I say, "EXCRUCIATING!"

My wrist was put in a splint and I was awarded "The Collar of Shame" to hold my neck steady while the C-5 healed. Then the docs gave me the ultimate New Years Eve gift…"Legal Drugs!!!." Yes they gave me the 1989 equivalent of Oxycontin, in ongoing tablet form, to help ease my pain through the next week.

Before all this happened, we had been planing to attend the New Years Eve service at the Schaumburg Church of the Nazarene. Even in my drug induced state of euphoria, I insisted that we all pile in the van and go to church. The reason for my enthusiasm, was that the Pastor told us he had arranged for the praise team from an A.M.E. Chicago church to come out and lead us in worship to welcome the New Year.

This group did not disappoint! They brought their own Hammond Organ, with Leslie Tone Cabinet, a five piece rock band with three gals who could wail out the lyrics! Their harmonies and dance moves reminded me of Ray Charles' "Raylets"!

I lay on my back at the back of the church, reveling in the throbbing bass line, reverberating through the floor and the soaring strains of the Leslie Tone cabinet lifting the praise and worship to heights which I had never previously experienced. I had not even felt this level of euphoria at the Grateful Dead concerts in Candlestick Park, which I had attended in a similarly supine and drug induced state, back in the Seventies.

In short, it was the best New Years Eve party I have ever attended, before or since. The drugs might have had something to do with it, but I prefer to give credit to God, the bass guitar, the ladies vocal back up, and the Leslie Tone Cabinet.

I could have broken my neck and been like Christopher Reeves, who sustained a severed spinal cord and was in a wheelchair for the rest of his life. You may recall, Reeves fell from his horse, during a riding competition, striking his head at a ninety degree angle to the ground, from his horseback position. Ouch, crunch! Reeves' accident was similar to mine, in that I hit the immovable object with a similar force, but from horizontal angle, while Reeves hit it vertically. I suspect the forces were similar.Again, I have no idea why the Lord spared me from paralysis or death. Perhaps because He knew the kids we had just adopted would have preferred a Daddy who would play outdoor games with them, rather than simply offering them rides on his wheelchair.

When I get to Heaven, I will ask Him questions about all these things. Maybe not. As "Mercy Me" once wrote:"I can only imagine."

4) While I was working as a "Technical Marketing Specialist" for AMP incorporated, I was assigned a territory in the Midwest which included Illinois, Indiana, Michigan, Minnesota, Missouri, and Wisconsin. It was my job to travel and train the local sales engineers and their clients about the use of our new "high tech" connector products. I held seminars and sales meetings. I held forth eloquently at trade shows, assisted by the latest in still

pictorial technology, my Kodak Carousel Projector and its round slide trays.

I once was told about the difference between an "expert" and an "authority." The expert had performed a procedure or given a lecture ten or more times. The "authority" would also have performed at least ten times, but also would have traveled over fifty miles to share his insights, and have a Carousel slide tray with a projector in his hands to illustrate his points.

In one of these "high tech" voyages, where I could demonstrate my "authority," I had traveled to Milwaukee, Wisconsin. This was my last stop in a multi-State tour before I returned to my home base in Chicago, Illinois. My local salesman was a young man with whom I had spent the previous afternoon and evening. We had taken one of his customers out to dinner.

Our final appointment ended before noon. My flight back to Chicago was not until 1:45P.M. My salesman suggested we have lunch and a "few Beverages" at a local establishment near the Airport which featured "scantily clad" ladies. I said, "O.K., but we have to watch our time."

After a few beverages and a sandwich, I said we needed to leave. He assured me, "we have plenty of time." The airport was only a ten-minute drive, at most. This was before the era of TSA and luggage checks, so arriving ten minutes ahead of departure at the gate was not an "unheard of choice."

But as the time continued to unravel, along with the items of clothing the women wore, I insisted he drive me to the airport. After much hesitation, he did get me out to the car and we "sort of sped" to the Airport.

Having checked the departure gate for my flight, I am now running, with my slide projector case in one hand and my suitcase in the other, to get there before the Gate closed. I did not make it.

The person at the gate told me my flight had just pulled away and there was no way for me to board. "But couldn't you call the pilot and have him just stop the plane? Couldn't you have them drop the staircase? I could run out on the tarmac and get on board!"

Obviously, these were the ravings of a madman, unwilling to tell his wife and children that he was three hours late coming home because of "Business Schedule Delays." These delays were "not our fault" but rather involved young women whom the devil had assigned to both stimulate and embarrass us."The devil made me do it!," as Flip Wilson used to say in his comedy routines. I didn't believe that my wife would be pleased to hear this excuse.

But, as the Gate attendant regarded me with a gaze, normally reserved for the mentally challenged, she replied simply, "No sir. That is not possible."

I skulked over to the large observation windows next to the departure gate and watched with fury building in my heart, as my plane taxied toward the runway for departure. I continued to watch as the plane was called for its turn to take off. As the plane accelerated down the runway towards its last leg of the journey to Chicago, the plane suddenly nosedived into the woods and burst into flame! WOW.

All of a sudden, I was so happy for my lustfully indulgent salesman. I was so happy for the airline rules which would not allow a tardy passenger to run out on the tarmac to board. I was so happy that no one would "break the rules" to deprive the plane of its timely "appointed rounds."

At the next moment, was I loudly proclaiming, "Thanks be to The Lord, who just saved my life!" in front of all the passengers assembled at that window? No, I simply said to anyone within earshot, while pointing through the window,"I was supposed to be on that plane!"

I don't recall if anyone who heard my statement of fact said, "Wow, you were sure lucky!" Or, if there were any Believers in the house, they may have said, "God bless you, brother! God must have a greater plan in mind for your life!"

But I don't recall any such comments, at all. I do remember calling my wife in Chicago and saying to her, "Honey, I have good news and bad news." (she always hated when I said that). "I was delayed getting to the airport on time, but as a result of my being late, I missed my flight. The flight I would have been on crashed and burned at the end of the runway."

"So what's the bad news,?'" she asked. " I'll be home a couple of hours late." I innocently replied.

Have you ever noticed that when there is an emergency, particularly one in which your life is spared, no one ever asks, "Well, what were you doing that made you late?" Everyone, almost naturally, assumes that it was "God's will and divine intervention" that made you late.

Of course, there were other occasions where I had acted against the intention of my marriage vows. These occasions, when added up, ultimately led to my second marriage ending in divorce.

Was I still "saved" from death or serious injury even though I went to the shows that made me late, as referenced above? Was I feeling "justified" that I had attended these shows? After all, it could be argued by a Dicey Theologian (The D.T. degree in Theology), that by attending the shows, my life had been spared. But I don't think that attending "strip shows" is one of God's preferred methods for protecting people's lives. Or, maybe it is. I'll have to ask when I get to the Golden Gates; He **does** have a great sense of humor!

On a more serious note, I think of those folks who were late to work in the Twin Towers on 9/11. Their tardiness, God ordained or not, also enabled them to avoid death in a burning building.

Burning buildings are not the fault of the employees. But, why would God save any of us from our own stupidity? A number of people in NYC went back into the burning building or the building next door thinking everything would be O.K. Does He always have a "higher Purpose in mind," for each and every one of us? I have noticed on many occasions that God has a sense of humor which is often beyond my understanding. These events in my life, as well as the Duck Boat incident and the the people who avoided death in Twin Towers lead me to wonder. Does God have a "Double Standard?" What are God's standards for my behavior" after I come to Him through Jesus? Is God personally responsible for whoever lives and dies? and Does my behavior influence His decisions in any way?

This question may be an erroneous one that misses a major point of our relationship with God, as Believers in Jesus. We'll explore it more in the next chapter.

Chapter 6

God's Standards - Are they "Double"

When I signed up as a volunteer for the U.S. Army in 1968, I didn't know that I was signing up to be under another standard than the one in which I had grown up. When I became a believer and said, "Yes Jesus I accept you as the Lord and King of my life."I didn't know that I was signing up for a different legal standard.

The Kingdom of Heaven has its own laws, it's own economy. It's like my being in the Army where there was the UCMJ standard for the military and the State and National laws outside the Military for everyone else. We had the PX where we could buy the same things offered outside, but they were much less expensive. Does God have a "Double Standard" one for believers and one for non-believers? Are there two sets of Laws? I believe God does have a "Double Standard. One may rightly conclude that under Grace, the "New Covenant," we are no longer held to the standards of "The Law of Moses" for our relationship with the Creator of the Universe. It's a radical concept indeed that unlike being under "Religion," under Grace our behavior shouldn't not count anymore, at least not as far as God is concerned. Let's explore that concept here.

We have seen before in Hebrews Isaiah and elsewhere that we are forgiven of all our sins, ("missing the mark") by our Father in Heaven. We have seen further in Hebrews, that Jesus "ever makes intercession for us."(Hebrews7:25 KJV)

We are "saved" by our acceptance of Jesus death on the cross and His ressurection for us. We trust in Him as our gateway to eternal life with God. Yet, in addition, Hebrews says that Jesus is "ever making intercession for me." The writer of Hebrews must have had me in mind. I certainly needed Jesus intercession for me on an ongoing basis.

Can we lose our salvation for our errant behavior? Many of us were taught in the churches of our youth, that salvation **was** just temporary. Not in so many words, mind you, but from the instructions we received after our salvation, it was clear we were expected to believe salvation was temporary, absent our "self redeeming works."

When we confess and receive Jesus "once and for all" sacrifice and ressurection for us; now we have "salvation." Yet many contend that continued peace with God is dependent on what we do - or don't, do or say. Some in the churches in which we were raised would say, "By Grace are you saved but you'd better do, 'at least the Ten Commandments' to continue with God's immutable, unconditional and reckless love!"On the face of it, that declaration makes no sense.

As we've seen earlier, Ephesians, Galatians, Hebrews, Romans and others all tell us we are saved by our faith, not by our works. Hebrews tells us we are preserved in our living relationship with God, by Jesus constantly making intercession for us with The Father. Romans tells us that there are no powers which can successfully come against us, because of our relationship with God.

We are told,"My little children, I am writing these things to you so that you may not sin. But if anyone does sin, we have an advocate with the Father, Jesus Christ the righteous."(1 John 2:1 ESV)

Summarizing the Gospel of Grace; Jesus died on the cross a sacrificial death for all of us, once and for all sin. As we believe on Him and accept His sacrifice for us, or "as us," we are forgiven for all time. Our "Spirit Man" is even seated in Heavenly places next to Jesus right now!(Ephesians 2:6)

The most amazing part of the Gospel of Grace is that God even forgets that we have ever refused relationship with Him. He forgets there was a time where we literally "had no time for Him" in our lives.

How is God's brain "wired" that He can forget? We are made in His image, but humans have a very persistent memory. Can you imagine, for instance, a conversation between God and Jesus as they sit next to each other in the Throne Room of Heaven?

Jesus is turning towards The Father saying,"Dad do we forgive Jack for making a stupid choice, going to that "Gentleman's Club?" The Father says, 'When did he do that? You know I forgot all that, and so did you.' Jesus says, 'Did I just ask you a question about Jack?' God says,'I can't remember.'"

Could Heavenly conversations really be like that? As I've mentioned before, in the Word God says,"I will be merciful toward their iniquities and **I will remember their sins no more.**"(Heb 8:12 ESV) As an old refrigerator magnet I had used to put up the kid's crayon drawings, once proclaimed, "The Bible says it. I believe it!" It may seem impractical or even impossible, but I believe what the Word says about God's memory.

However, I **do** think Father and Son **do** remember the beneficial stuff we do. That would be great because the Bible also says that there will be rewards in Heaven. Matthew 16, for instance, tells us,"For the Son of Man (Jesus) is going to come with His

Angels in the glory of His Father; and then He will **recompense** each person according to what he has done."(Matt 16:27 ESV) If that's so, then God has to remember the "good stuff' we did, so He can justly reward us in Heaven. But the "stupid stuff," it's as though it never happened. That's logical, isn't it? I like the "odds" on those rewards. The good we do counts towards the rewards, the bad stuff is forgotten.

There is no doubt that God is amazingly forgiving toward us, and that brings up the question of what is God's standard for our forgiveness toward others? Jesus tells Peter in Matthew to forgive others of their sins against us…"Seventy times seven"(Matt 18:21). Even the "iniquities" (the personal sins they committed on purpose)?Do they have to come to us and beg our forgiveness? Do we have the right to engage them in deep conversation about why they would have done something so stupid? Does God pardon us even without our asking Him to forgive us for acting stupid? Will God continue to "rail on us" about our stupidity?

I have examined Psalm 103 in detail. Remember this is "Old Testament." But, I love the language with which King David expresses himself in this Psalm."The Lord is merciful and gracious, slow to anger and abounding in lovingkindness. He will not always strive with us, nor will he keep His anger forever. He has not dealt with us according to our sins (missing the mark, or standard), trespasses (crossing a known relational barrier) nor repay us with punishment according to our iniquities (<u>intentional,</u> premeditated rejection of friendship with God, which are even repeated).Parentheses are mine(Psalm 103:8-10AMP)

King David believes God will forgive all three categories of separation from God's will in Psalm 32. "I acknowledged my sin to You, and did not cover my iniquity. I said, 'I will confess my transgressions to The Lord.'" (Ps 32:5 ESV)

Back in Psalms 103 David recognizes the extent of God's forgiveness. "For as high as the Heavens are above the Earth, so great is His steadfast love toward those who fear Him, as far as the East is from the West, so far does He remove our transgressions (a violation of the Law) from us. As a father shows compassion to His children, so the Lord shows compassion to those who fear Him. For He knows our frame and remembers that we are dust." (Psalm 103:11-14 ESV) David reminds God here that He was the scientist who created us imperfect. He should remember, then, that we were created from dust. One's expectations of "dust" should likely be very small.

Do we even have to "beg God to forgive us for our stupidity," intentional or otherwise? I see nothing in this passage to indicate that is a necessity. Does the Bible tell us that we must forgive others who have offended us, even though they have not "begged our forgiveness?" I believe it does.

Regarding God's forgiveness of us and how that reflects on our behavior, let's look at Matthew 18. In response to Peter's question, "How many times should I forgive my enemies? Jesus tells Peter he should forgive his enemies "seventy times seven times," not just the seven required by the Law of Moses. (Matt 18:21-22 KJV)

Then Jesus goes on to relate the story of how the Kingdom of Heaven is like a King who wanted to settle debts with his servants. One servant was brought in, "who owed him ten thousand bags of gold (or Ten Thousand Talents)." In todays economy that would have been Three Billion Dollars (U.S.)! The

King was going to take all the servant's property, his wives and children and throw him in prison until the debt should be repaid.

At this point it is interesting to me, that the servant did not beg the King to forgive his debt, he merely asked for more time to pay it back. "The servant fell down and worshipped him saying,'Lord have patience with me and I will pay thee all.' Then the Lord of that servant was moved with compassion, and loosed him and forgave the debt." (Matt 18:23-27 KJV).

Imagine that: even <u>without</u> the servant begging for forgiveness, simply by the servant admitting that he <u>did</u> owe the king the money and being accountable. He merely asked if he could only have more time, he would surely repay the King all that he owed. The servant didn't even have to fill out a contract agreeing to monthly payments. The King simply forgave the debt!

Jesus is telling this story to His disciples to emphasize how important forgiveness is in the Kingdom of Heaven. I've heard people say of someone who offended them,"I would forgive them, but they never apologized, nor asked me to forgive them." Must we be like that King and forgive, even without an apology, even without asking for forgiveness? Is God like that to us?

Think of it today, what's the likelihood of "a servant," repaying millions of dollars? Was the King simply writing off the debt because he knew it could never be repaid? Does God, our King, write off our debt for Jesus death on the cross because He knows it can never be repaid.? Now wait just a minute. Jesus Death on the Cross repaid our debt to God for the sin in our lives. So we have no more debt to God. But there is one "debt we still have". We will get to it later.

What kind of money would the servant have had under his personal control? What would his Equifax score have been for any institution to loan that kind of money in the first place? The King was doubtless being generous with his servant to begin with, as God is generous with us.

I remember when I asked my mother to loan me Two Thousand Dollars to put a down payment on my first house (this was 1976). She replied,"I will give you the money. I don't want you feeling that you owe me something."

When we are part of the family, we may get unexpected gifts. As believers, we are part of God's family and we sometimes receive what Graham Cooke calls "suddenlies." God sends us those unexpected gifts or occurrences which can change our direction in life.

So Jesus is comparing God's love for us and forgiveness of our sins (perhaps, unintentional slips) and iniquities (intentional disobedience) to this King's forgiveness of the debt of his servant?

Forgiveness is the purpose of Jesus' lesson. But later, Jesus tells us,"that same servant went out and found one of his fellow servants, which owed him a hundred pence (about Five Thousand Dollars, U.S.):and he laid hands on him, took him by the throat, saying,'Pay me that thou owest!' And his fellow servant fell down at his feet and besought him saying, "Have patience with me and I will pay thee all."(Matt 18:28-30 KJV)

This was the identical situation that the formerly mentioned servant had with the King. Yet, in this case the "forgiven servant" would not accept his fellow servant's request for "patience" and has the servant who owes him money thrown into prison.

Of course this is not done in secret. The fellow servants report the problem to the King. The King calls back the "forgiven servant" calls him a "wicked servant" and turns him over to the "tormentors" (Matt 18:32-35 KJV)

The moral of Jesus' story and similar stories, which He tells elsewhere, is "forgive as you have been forgiven." God has given us a gift of unimaginable worth (thus the analogy of "Ten Thousand Gold Talents" above) in His sacrifice for us through Jesus. That priceless gift permits us to be forgiven of our sins. Under Old Testament Law bulls and goats were offered as sacrifices every year, but they were only a "covering for sin".Jesus sacrifice as our Savior removed our sin and cleared our relationship with God "once and for all"(Heb 10:10 ESV).

If we do not forgive, then we can't be surprised if life turns against us. After Jesus death and ressurection, we as believers, will not have lost our salvation because of something stupid we do or say, that's between us and God. In His eyes we are the "Righteousness of God in Christ"(2 Cor 5:21 NASB) as believers, trusting in the salvation Jesus won for us.

However, our earthly relationships will certainly be damaged by our deeds and by our unforgiveness. We may even develop disabilities and illnesses in our own bodies as a result of the bitterness stored in our souls, due to unforgiveness.

Some of you may feel my last musings here in these pages are "Heresy." For those who tend to feel that we can "lose our salvation through bad behavior," I empathize. I too, once believed that.

When I was in the Nazarene Church. I would have to go forward each week and confess any new sins against God to one of the

Deacons at the altar. One Deacon got so exasperated by my coming up every week, that he would simply sigh and drop his shoulders when he saw me coming. I couldn't cover up my iniquities, I felt obligated to confess them and square accounts with God. If I didn't, I might "Die in my Sins" (any which were unconfessed) and be immediately assigned to the "Hot Spot" and I don't mean Phoenix, Arizona.

However, these passages and others like it, remind us that Jesus, by His own free will, was crucified and resurrected, "once for all,"and that "by that will, we have been sanctified (made Holy) through the offering of the body of Jesus Christ.(Hebrews 10:10 ESV)

The Word tells us that Jesus sacrifice was more than an "atonement," where one is sacrificed to cover another. "Atonement" was the case under the Old Covenant, where bulls and goats were sacrificed for our sins. But in Jesus case, he didn't die "for our sins," then He would have had to die again every year after that as more sin was comitted, as the bulls did. Rather he died "as us, for us," just one time, as though it were we ourselves hanging on that cross.

The Law of Moses showed us in no uncertain terms that we could not be Holy by merely obeying "some" of the Six Hundred Thirteen Laws of the Mosaic Covenant. The book of James tells us that,"the person who keeps all the laws except one, is as guilty as a person who has broken all of God's Laws."(James 2:10 NLT).

We have no hope in the "natural." Thinking we are O.K. because we try to obey the Ten Commandments and because we say "we love Jesus." We say we have been "saved by His

Grace," but what if we "don't act like it"? Then what will God do to us? We may doubt our eternal destination!

When we try to mix Mosaic Law with God's Grace, we Christians (except Seventh Day Adventists) are "dead in the water from the git go," because we worship on Sundays. Under Mosaic Law, Saturday was the Holy Day, the Sabbath. We have already erred by The Law of Moses. Well, if you think that's pretty unreasonable of God, not to let us change the Sabbath, then Jesus made it even harder for us in Matthew 5!

Jesus redefined the impact of the "Ten" by saying, "you have heard it said to those of old. 'You shall not murder, and whoever murders will be liable to judgment.' But I say unto you, everyone who is angry with his brother will be liable to judgement." (Matt 5:21-22 ESV) And if that weren't enough, then Jesus continues to advise those assembled on the mountain that "everyone who looks at a woman with lustful intent has already committed adultery with her in his heart."(Matt 5:28 ESV). Whoops!

By Jesus definitions in Matthew, God not only holds us to the Old Testament rules of "right behavior" but even "right intent"! How could a mere mortal be held to these standards in order to be accepted by God for Eternal Life with Him? A dilemma to be sure.

But wait, there's an answer that God created! Through Jesus sacrifice, by His living and dying "as us," we would no longer be held accountable for any of our sins, past, present, or future. Jesus only had to die once for us, and like Him, our "Spirit Man" dies once with Him. Then we are "reborn" with the new Holy Spirit living within us! We are baptized to symbolize our death and ressurection with Jesus.

Under Mosaic Law, when the bull was sacrificed, the bull was rigorously examined by the Priest. If the bull were found to be without defect, then the priest would sacrifice the bull, to pay for our sins. That sacrifice was only good for a year, then another sacrifice would have to be made. <u>However</u>, the sacrifice was not for **past sins; it was for the sins we would commit in the coming year**. Imagine that! The foundations of Grace were apparent even in the rituals of Mosaic Law!

But, unlike the sacrifices of bulls and goats, when we accept Jesus sacrifice, "as us," it is as though we become a different person. We become like Christ, not that we are instantly made perfect, but that we now have the Holy Spirit living and working in us, which we did not have in our "pre-Christ" existence. In the Old Covenant the people had Prophets who would give them God's guidance. Under the New Covenant, we have the Holy Spirit (God) living in us. We don't have to go to the Temple, to commune with God, we **are** the Temple. He lives within us!

"Therefore if anyone is in Christ, he is a new creation; the old things have passed away; behold all things have become new."(2 Corinthians 5:17 NKJV). We further see evidence of our transformation in Ephesians 4, "and to put on the new self, which in the likeness of God has been created in righteousness and holiness of the truth."(Eph :4:24 NASB)

In our transformation through our faith and belief, through our acknowledgment that Christ died as us, and that as He was resurrected from the grave, so, we too, are resurrected into a new life. Much like the caterpillar going into his cocoon, we emerge as a completely different creature in Christ. But, unlike the butterfly, we don't look all that different on the outside. Yet on the inside, we are totally different and "brand new."

In the 2019 movie, <u>Breakthrough</u>, the true story is told of a sixteen-year-old boy who falls through the ice, playing with friends on a school holiday. This boy attends church, with his parents, but really has no particular ties to church or God. He is rescued by firemen and is transported to a local medical clinic.

Unfortunately, too much time had passed while he was underwater. It appears by the readings of all life indicators that the boy is deceased. He is "flatlined." The doctor waits to pronounce him "clinically dead" until his mother can get there to hear what he has to say. In response to the doctor's statement, "There's nothing more we can do." The mother begins crying out that the Holy Spirit should immediately rise up and revive her son, which He apparently does. The medical instruments begin beeping merrily away and while the boy is still unconscious. His life has been miraculously restored!

In the movie, it is shown that God in "His mercy and Grace," has allowed other people to die. The young man's teacher asks him, point-blank, "Why would God let my husband die of an aneurysm and let you live?" His friends call him "Miracle Boy" and ask him, "Why would God let others die, and yet you live? Does God have something special for you?" Good question!

In writing this book, I have pondered God's purposes for my life and others. I have recently come to the conclusion that God's whole purpose in letting some live and others die is to simply build our faith. These events also give Glory to God through those who are saved and those who are "left behind". If the folks who died were believers (and who but God is to say that they were, or were not) then we know they are going to a "better place than here." Who are we, among those"left behind" to deny our loved ones a place at the banquet table in Heaven?

God's plan in sparing our lives, so that we **are** left behind. may be simply to convince us again and again that He loves us beyond measure. He loves us beyond the value of Ten Thousand Talents.

If we play the Lottery every week, and never win, God want's us to know that, in His "Big Picture," we are so loved that he not only sent His son to die for us, so that we could have eternal life, <u>He sent His son, not to condemn us but to save the world with us and through us.</u> We are literally "the body of Christ" as the Church today. In itself, that is certainly a great purpose! We don't have to be famous like Billy Graham or Mother Teresa, we can be the "only Bible they know" to people with whom we interact. This an important calling God has for all of us, Ordained or not! We have noted this earlier In Jeremiah 29:11 God's "Plan and purpose," along with the "hope for the future" is what He gives all of us.

Now if God always has a plan to build our faith, and "If God is all-powerful AND always in control, then why do bad things happen?" Does God cause cancer to "teach us a lesson"? I think not! That would be called "Child Abuse" by our Earthly authorities. I have noted earlier that when loved ones are "taken from us" in death, our response is often to be "angry with God"

Let's look at Rabbi Harold Kushner who wrote the book: <u>When Bad Things Happen to Good People</u>,*(Random House Pub., 1981).* The book was written a few years after the death of his son, at age fourteen, of an incurable disease. Looking back on the events and his own heart, Rabbi Kushner saw he could not have done anything to offend God. At least, not to the point that God would require the death of Kushner's son to "set things straight" between them. Kushner said he did not believe God was punishing him. Instead, Kushner's point of view, as expressed in his book, is that God will always "do His best" and is "always with us in our suffering," but there IS "a limit as to what He is <u>able to do</u> to prevent it."

When the book came out, many Orthodox Jews and Evangelical Christians thought the book was antithetical to the Gospel and Jewish Law. Many thought it was "heretical" to claim that God had insufficient power to intervene in a crisis. They criticized Kushner's expressed point of view of a "**limited God.**"

On the other hand, I believe Kushner was right. God is limited. Indeed, He has limited Himself. He wanted us to see that we couldn't do anything we wanted to on our own, rather, like Jesus "the Son can do nothing on His own accord, but only what He sees the Father doing. For whatever the Father does, that the Son does likewise."(John 5:19.ESV)

It might have something to do with the Creation Laws of the Universe, and The Law of Love. These laws have nothing to do with the "Law of Moses," they are like the Law of Gravity and the Aerodynamic Law of Lift. Regardless of our beliefs, absent any external devices which might give our bodies "Lift," we are all going to fall to the ground when we jump off a tall building.

Is it God's will that we die from jumping off a building? No, God doesn't wish anyone to perish, nor to be ill. In fact The Apostle John states that it is God's desire that we, "may prosper, in all things, and be in health, just as your soul prospers." (3 John 2 NKJV) But, at the same time, we all must obey the Laws of Physics by which God created the Universe, or suffer the physical consequences.

What about "The Law of Love"? How could "love" allow anyone to be hurt or die? Good question! It's because the heart of the definition of the word "love" is "choice." Daddy God will not violate the choice which Daddy has given all of us to live and choose as we wish. Otherwise we would be like the Israelites in Egypt. We would be slaves to a dictator, however nice he might be.

God says in James "if any of you lacks wisdom, let him ask of God who gives to all generously and without reproach, and it will be given to him." (James 1:5 NASB) So, if I don't ask, and I go ahead with my own plans based on the "desires of my flesh" without checking with Daddy first…what might be the consequences? My question might be as simple as asking,"What's up today Daddy?" There might be a more complex issue having to do with family plans or business plans where it's not just me asking or choosing, but a larger group of souls looking to choose.

My wife Jan often reminds me that I should choose "consequential thinking" when making a decision. It's her way of reminding me that I should always seek God.

Not all of us DO ask God. Not every time, and some of us, "not ever."
I certainly don't <u>always</u> ask Him, probably most of the time to my detriment. By not asking and receiving, I limit the manifestation of what good God has already planned for me.

As noted above from the book of Jeremiah, God says," For I know the plans I have for you, declares the Lord, plans for welfare and not for evil, to give you a future and a hope." (Jeremiah 29:11 ESV) In this verse God says HE knows, but <u>we</u> do not know His plans, until we ask Him.

When we ignore the promptings of the Holy Spirit or fail to ask God for wisdom, we may miss God's Best for us. The consequences of not seeking God are usually not a "disaster," but quite often, we DO miss God's best for us.

As I look back on my own life, as well as the history of the Israelites, I see that God **does** appear to have a double standard. One for the people who have come to Him for salvation and eternal peace and another for those who deny Him a place in their hearts. The irony of human life is that God does not deny **anyone** his wisdom and His blessing. It is always **our choice** of what we are willing to believe and what we are willing to receive, even up unto the moment of our last breath.

We should truly take the advice of Paul in Phillipians 4 to give God thanks and glory in all things, even when the situation looks awful. It is not just Norman Vincent Peale who advises always having a positive outlook. The most highlighted verses in the Kindle version of the Bible are these, according to data released by Amazon," Do not be anxious about anything, but in every situation, by prayer and petition, with thanksgiving present your requests to God, And the peace of God, which transcends all understanding will guard your hearts and minds in Christ Jesus."(Phil 4:617 NIV)

On this note, however, you may remember the series of photos shot by Associated Press Photographer, Richard Drew of a falling man on 9/11. (Esquire Magazine Sept 9, 2016, details the pictures and events in a story by Tom Junod, titled "The Falling Man, an Unforgettable Story"). In those photos we see a man in a white shirt and black pants and black boots falling against the background of the North Tower. His body appears relaxed. His one leg is straight, the other is casually bent. His white shirt, or jacket, is billowing out as he falls head first. As the fall continues, in the twelve photos taken, we see an orange undershirt appear. If he has any concerns for the consequences which would arise from his hitting the pavement a few moments later, they do not show in his physical expressions, or movements.

I believe from the photographic evidence, that he is at peace with the impending end of his life. I would say he has no regrets. I know that's a lot to assume from twelve sequential photos, but it could well be the same physical expression of peace that you or I might feel if we were literally "falling into the Arms of God." By the way, I am not fond of heights in the first place.

When we are in the midst of a disaster or when we are spared the consequences of a disaster of our own making, we should recall Philippians 4:6 and 7. Praise God, lift up His holy name and thank Him for the opportunity of honoring Him in our stories and with our lives. Those are our testimonies. This book is my testimony. We should give God all the Glory and not ourselves nor another person. I hope I have done that here.

Like Eating Jelly With Chop Sticks   Jack Narvel

Chapter 7

The Gospel of Condemnation - Why it is so popular?

If, as in the last chapter, the good stuff **and** the bad stuff, is **NOT** on the shoulders of an all-powerful and benevolent God, then maybe it's on all of us! It may well be our own choices, conscious or unconscious that determine our fate.

We anticipate the praise we will get when the "game is over" and we have defeated the other teams. We get awards we can place on our mantles! Of course, there is also "the agony of defeat" ("The Thrill of Victory…the Agony of Defeat" - ABC Sports). You may remember the video ABC ran with it - a runner crossing the finish line, and a skier wiping out and tumbling down the hill. Whoopee! Jan and I love to watch the Olympics.

Competitive sports are very popular, but not with everyone. Some people prefer a quiet game where everyone just interacts and there are no winners and losers. I often wonder why the world can't be like that.

I remember when some friends of ours asked us to join them in playing "The Non-Game Game." The wife was in the hospital, recovering in bed from surgery, so the idea of a stressful competitive game was not something the husband desired for her. So he brought "The Non-game Game" to her hospital room. I had never heard of it before that time.

The phrase "Non-Game game," according to Wikipedia, "was originally coined by the late President of Nintendo, Satoru Iwata, who described it as "a form of entertainment that really doesn't have a winner or even a real conclusion." Wikipedia goes on to say: "the main difference between non-games and traditional video games is the lack of structured goals objectives and challenges. This allows the player a greater degree of self-expression through free-form play since he or she can set up his or her own goals to achieve."

The game was not a video game in those days, it was a board game with dice and character markers. As I recall, we didn't enjoy playing the game nearly as much as the wife did. She set her goals without telling us, and she says she achieved them! Hooray, good game! Thanks for playing! But, according to the "rules" of the "Non-game Game," you don't even have to tell the other players your goals, unless you want to.

Jan and I are very competitive people. We need to set goals and accomplish them in life and on the card table. We need to know the reasons why we were unsuccessful so we can "do better next time."

We have this sense that as human beings, we must be doing SOMETHING. We should **not be like cats** who spend all day just sleeping and being petted (when they desire to be petted) with pauses to eat and play with a ball of tin foil, or catnip mouse. Rather we should be busy doing some activity. We should be doing it better and better in order to be like the professional athletes whom we see on television.

After all, doesn't Paul say,"Do you not know that in a race all runners run, but only one receives the prize? So run that you may obtain it."(1 Cor 9:24 ESV) As Christians we may feel we must "run" to serve God, almost "in competition with one another" in order to obtain and keep God's Grace.

Aren't Mother Teresa and Billy Graham elevated to and "entitled to" that "special place of God's unending Love for all Eternity?" Of course they are! Look at all they have "done for God." But I am certainly not! I have not made nearly enough "sacrifices" to qualify.

I don't mean sacrifices of Bulls and Goats, that's what the Israelites did to be worthy of God's love in the Old Testament. No, today our sacrifices should be of our time, our spiritual gifts and our finances in order to be worthy of God's Love and Mercy and Grace. But perhaps even that's not what God intended for us, after we accept Christ and His forgiveness for our sins. Let's look further into God's heart for us as we re-visit the Israelites in the desert.

As believers today, we have that sense of obligation and competitiveness in common with the Israelites. When they came out of slavery in Egypt. They were in the desert, on their way to the Promised Land. The Israelites had been slaves of the Egyptians. They had impossible quotas of bricks and "Pyramid building work" to do in order obtain the "Grace of Pharaoh."

Apparently, they were well fed, in Egypt, because they complain to Moses later about how they had given up all this great food they used to have; now they have "manna" instead. But they had forgotten that aside from the food, they had to live under the whip of a harsh and unforgiving dictator. As they fled Egypt, they apparently expected God to be the same. That is, a dictator, however benevolent, who would require certain things of them.

That was not the God of Israel. Their God was loving and merciful, but they weren't getting the message. He realized he needed to show them something more substantial than "the parting of the Red Sea," in order for them to truly get the magnitude of His Power and His love for His Nation.

Let's look at what he did in Exodus. This is one of my favorite Bible stories and I only discovered it recently!

In Exodus 33 the story is told of how God and Moses had a relationship as friends. "Thus the LORD used to speak to Moses' face to face, as a man speaks to his friend." (Exodus 33:11 ESV) All well, and good, but what about the rest of "His Nation?"

In Exodus 19, we see that God intended to be more than just a friend to Moses. He wanted to be close with all the Israelites, and even all of us today. Let's see how this plays out. It was God's intention that the Israelites become a "Kingdom of Priests" to share the love of God with other Nations. We see in Exodus 19 through 24, that the Israelites were still stuck in their "Egyptian Slave Mentality." They wanted to be free from Pharaoh's oppression, but they did not get that they could be priests, not slaves. Nor did they get that was what God desired for them.

Please turn with me in your Bibles to Exodus 19. It starts by God creating an amazing thunderstorm at the base of Mount Sinai. That's a great beginning to a story isn't it? **"It was a dark and stormy night."** Thunder lightning, trumpets loudly blaring, WOW! On the first day of the third month after the Israelites left Egypt, they came to the foot of Mount Sinai. God then called up his friend Moses and told him to gather the Israelites and tell them "Now, therefore, if you obey my voice and keep my covenant, you shall be my treasured possession among all peoples ….**You will be a kingdom of priests and a holy nation.**"(Exodus 19:5-6 ESV)

The Lord told Moses to have the people consecrate themselves to be ready for a meeting at the foot of Mount Sinai where The LORD would appear to them. "Because on that third day, The Lord would come down on Mount Sinai in the sight of all the people." (Exodus 19:11 ESV)

If you consider it for a moment, it is amazing that God, who just a little while before this meeting ,would never let Himself be seen, not even by Moses. Yet, He now decides to show Himself, in plain sight to the gathered Israelites. After they had washed their clothes and "purified themselves" for the third day, they waited. This was the day God had appointed for Himself to reveal His Glory."

Oh, the anticipation they must have felt and even the fears they must have felt, knowing that God was about to **speak** personally to them, and even **appear** to them. What would He look like? What would God speaking personally to them sound like? At this time, the Israelites had no point of reference. They had seen the miracles God performed for them in Egypt and the parting of the Red Sea as they were leaving, but they had not seen God personally or heard His voice.

Remember, just like the leper in the previous chapter, The Israelites still had a "slave mentality." They considered themselves lowly and subordinate. They never fought for themselves.They needed clear instruction as to how to conduct themselves, so that "The Master" might be pleased. Moses knew what it was like to be a friend of God, and maybe Aaron did, but the rest of them hadn't a clue.

God wanted to free them from this "slave mindset." He wanted to show them that in His mind, they were His children. They were His Priests who would convey His Love to all the World.

Their future with God was to be very important. Let's look at what God does to show his power and His love and care for His people.

"On the morning of the third day, there were thunders and lightnings and a thick cloud on the mountain and a very loud trumpet blast so that all the people in the camp trembled. Then Moses led the people out of the camp to meet with God. They took their stand at the foot of the mountain. Mount Sinai was wrapped in smoke because the Lord had descended on it in the form of fire. The smoke of it went up like the smoke of a kiln and the whole mountain trembled greatly." (Exodus 19:16-18 ESV)

I don't know about you, but I love a good thunderstorm! When we planned our vacation to Hiawassee, Georgia last year, I was excited to read the forecast for our vacation week. There would be thunderstorms and rain ALL WEEK!I love a good thunderstorm, particularly in the mountains where the wind blows the tree limbs in cadence with the trickling sound of the raindrops on a tin roof. But in the Bible story, this was more than just "a good thunderstorm." The story goes on. "As the sound of the trumpet grew louder and louder, Moses spoke **and God answered him in thunder**." (Exodus 19:19 ESV)

As Pentecostal believers, we have heard of speaking in tongues and even done it ourselves. But imagine... speaking to God in tongues, or English or Aramaic or whatever language, and then, having God answer you with His voice of thunder! Unbelievable!

As the story continues, God spoke to Moses at the top of the mountain. God told Moses he should go back down, and bring Aaron up with him "Away! Get down and then come up, you and Aaron with you. But do not let the priests and the people break through to come up to the LORD, lest He break out against them."(Exodus 19:24 NKJV)

It's pretty clear that after God's loud display of power, no one but Moses would have wanted to "go up." But again, the Lord speaks privately to His friend Moses and the people are excluded.

And as we might expect, in that situation, the people stood well back from the base of the Mountain as God dictated the Six Hundred and Thirteen Commands to Moses. Then God told him to go back down the mountain and tell the people what He said. God had dictated to Moses the rules that would govern all aspects of their lives. How to treat each other, how to treat animals, how to treat strangers. Even dictating the time of day at which certain rules would apply.

But then something miraculous happens. As the Israelites are gathered at the foot of the Mountain, God Himself speaks to them directly, in a language they could understand. Not thunder, this time but in plain language The Lord gives them what would become the Ten Commandments, written on stone, by God Himself. In Exodus 20:1-17, we see God speaking directly to His people. He gives the Ten Commandments out loud.

Then, in Exodus 20:18, We see the people react to the spoken Word of God Himself."When the people heard the thunder and the loud blasts of the ram's horn, and when they saw flashes of lightning and the smoke billowing from the mountain, they stood at a distance, trembling with fear"(Ex 20:18 NLT)

Then came the first "review" of what it must have been like to hear God's voice directly. "And they said to Moses,' you speak to us, and we will listen. But don't let God speak to us, lest we die."(Ex 20:19 NLT)

Notice the shift here. God wants to speak to His people directly and does so. Yet the people have the idea that Moses has control over God. They assume in the forgoing passage that Moses had the power to control God.

Moses does't correct the people to say something like ,"God's just spoken to you plainly. He's never done that to a large group of people before. You guys are such Wussies. Now bow before Him and apologize!"

But that's not what Moses says to the people. Like a kindly grandfather comforting his children in the midst of a thunderstorm, Moses says,"Do not be afraid; for God has come to test you, and in order that the fear of Him may remain with you, so that you may not sin."(Ex 20:20 NASB). Moses tells them in essence,"Keep listening to Him. Don't be afraid of what He says or how He says it."

Naturally the people responded as you or I would today. "O.K. that's great! We just thought all that thunder and lightning was to kill us. Now that you've explained it, Moses, we know God is our loving Father, and we certainly want to spend more 'one on one' time with Him."

That's not what the Bible tells us. Instead,"The people stood far off, while Moses drew near to the thick darkness where God was." (Ex 20:21 ESV)

Then God speaks to Moses one on one, and reminds him that He has just personally spoken to His people. "Tell the Israelites this: 'you have seen for yourselves that I have spoken to you from Heaven.'" Then after reminding Moses that He has spoken the Ten Commandments to the Israelites personally, God continues through Exodus 23:33 to give the full text of the 613 Rules of Living to Moses, a second time.

At the end of this conversation with Moses, God says an amazing thing,"Come up to the Lord, you and Aaron, Nadab and seventy of the elders of Israel and worship Me from afar. Moses alone shall come near the Lord, but the others shall not come near and the people shall not come up with him." (Ex 24:1-2, ESV)

At that point Moses went down and told the people everything God had said. He quoted,"all the (613) rules. And all the people answered with one voice and said. 'all the words the Lord has spoken we will do.'"(Ex 24:3 ESV)

It's just as well there was no Facebook in that day. I can see the posts now: "that God of Moses, He only likes Moses. We're not 'good enough' to approach Him. God may be good, O.K., but I disagree with some of that stuff He said. I'd just like a 'One on One' without all that noise."Of course, today, under Grace, we **can** have quiet "one on One's with God." Thank you, Lord! We can even post our conversations with God on Facebook!

After speaking the words of God's covenant to the people, Moses then wrote these Six Hundred and Thirteen "Guidelines for Behavior," in a book, which he called "The Book of the Covenant." The next day, Moses offers burnt offerings to The Lord, and after completing the blood sacrifice ritual, Moses again reads the Book of the Covenant," In the hearing of the people. And they said 'All that the Lord has spoken we will do, and we will be obedient.'" (Exodus 24:7 NIV)

Now that God has spoken directly to His people, now that the Covenant has been confirmed twice with His people, God does a surprising thing. He invites Moses to bring up "Aaron, Nadab, Abihu and the seventy elders of Israel" to visit with Him personally and even have a meal with Him.

They went up on the mountain and God celebrated a covenant meal with them. WHAT? Just the day before anyone but Moses, who crossed the "Yellow God Tape" barrier would be destroyed. But now, it was all O.K.! God loved them and wanted to show them his love in a way they could understand. No lightning, no thunder, just something like an extravagant Church banquet after the service. Food and drink, as much as they wanted. Here's the details:

"Then Moses, Aaron, Abihu Joshua, Nadab and the seventy Elders of Israel climbed up the mountain. (Notice that God hadn't <u>specifically</u> invited Joshua, but he was Mo's assistant, so Moses brought him anyway.) **There they saw the God of Israel.** Under His feet there seemed to be a surface of brilliant blue lapis lazuli as clear as the sky itself. **And though these nobles of Israel gazed (directly) upon God, He did not destroy them. In fact, they ate a covenant meal, eating and drinking in His presence**." (Ex 24:9-11 NLT)

Here's the amazing part which tells us how God really wanted to interact with the Israelites then, and us today. Imagine you were an Elder in those days. There was no need to cover your eyes. You were invited to look directly upon the Holy One of Israel. Because you were a witness of God's Covenant, at this "Covenant Banquet," all of a sudden, it's O.K. to look upon God!

Was it even O.K. to fellowship with Him, directly? Perhaps even as Adam and Eve did in the Garden, or was it something short of that?

Let's imagine the scene: God has invited you to a meal along with the Pastor and all the Elders and Deacons in your church. Angels are coming to you as you are eating offering seconds refilling your wine glass, and asking,"Would you care for a cup of coffee with your cake?" or "Is everything prepared just the way you like it?" Would you say,"Oh yes, best ever!"? Or perhaps not even be able to speak? The Bible does not give us "A Heavenly Restaurant Review," but I'll bet it was a TEN Star (not just a Five Star) Michelin rating.

This is my idea of what the dinner party may have been like, but to be accurate, in light of other references from Ezekiel 1:26-28 and Revelation 5, <u>God was probably not seated at the table with them.</u> From these references, it is likely that Moses and the Elders were <u>looking up through the floor of God's throne room (the blue lapis lazuli) to the Throne of God, where God Himself was seated.</u>

At this time it may have been that the diners saw only God's feet and the base of His throne. It is not until the New Testament when Jesus affirms,"Have I been with all of you for so long a time, and do you not recognize and know me yet, Phillip? Anyone who has seen me has seen the Father, How can you say then, 'show us the Father?'"(John 14:9 AMPC)

But even if I had been unable to see anything but the base of God's throne and His feet, I would be thinking,"The food was 'out of this world!' This is truly a great and awesome God, who really loves us!"

My wife Jan says, "you are basing your idea of God's love shown in a 'Dinner Party for Israel' with just a few verses from Exodus." But it must be remembered that in Biblical times, and often today, when a contract is signed, all parties to the agreement celebrate the signing <u>with a meal.</u>

It was a big deal and surely worthy of a "Covenant Meal" when God gave this "Covenant of Moses" at that time and in the way He did. Nice dinner, great celebration and by the way, God, it was great to see you in person, if only your sandals and feet.

But aside from the great meal and the literal vision of God is there anything really great and worth noting in "The Covenant of Moses" compared to the "New Covenant" which Jesus brought?

The "Old Covenant," was "conditional." It puts the laws (all six hundred and thirteen) on us to obey. The "New Covenant" puts our relationship with God, <u>all on God</u> to do as He promises.

We should remember that at the time of Exodus 19-24, the Israelites were still of a slave mentality. Six Hundred Thirteen commands were a conditional covenant with God. Had they thought of themselves as Priests, they might have seen the Covenant differently," but as slaves, the Covenant was simply the orders of their "New Pharaoh" (God). They all said,"Yes, we will do all these things." But they had no idea what it would take to fulfill their promise.

Since Moses wrote all the books of the Pentateuch, and probably near the end of his life, scholars are not in agreement as to whether the books were sequential or put together on the basis of subject matter. But if the Israelites were unclear that the Covenant of Moses was indeed a conditional agreement with both blessings and cursing, dependent upon their behavior. Deuteronomy 28 and 29, makes it completely clear!

In those chapters, God declared that the "Covenant of Moses" was a **conditional agreement**. As the Israelites keep this covenant they would be blessed and as they broke this covenant they would be cursed. "Sorry God, we must have been napping when you said that stuff! Can we do a 're-boot?" For now, let's forget worrying about how we will do on our "Law Exam" and instead get back to the party.

I had missed this dinner party previously in my devotions. Did you know, prior to reading this, that God had a celebratory dinner for Moses and the Elders of Israel on Mount Sinai before He inscribed the Ten Commandments in stone? I have never heard a sermon on the significance of the dinner party on Mount Sinai. I think there should be one, but I won't preach it here.

O.K., I <u>will preach it here</u>, just a little bit. God wanted a relationship with Adam and Eve. God wanted a relationship with the Israelites. God wanted to bless his people. God had wanted the Israelites to be a "Kingdom of Priests," sharing God's love everywhere they went.

Yet throughout God's story in the Bible, we, both Gentiles and Jews, have rejected a direct relationship, as was enjoyed by Abraham, Moses, Noah and a few others. Those few exercised their God-given gift of choice to choose to partner with God. Many of us have not chosen to do that, even today under the "New Covenant."

Why is it then, even following this example of God's desire for direct fellowship in Exodus that we see the people choosing to appoint Moses and Aaron as their "Official Path to God." Why is it we choose to eat in dingy noodle restaurants? Maybe it is to simply associate with people who agree with us that we are unimportant. Why not accept our own importance to God and live as though we ARE important enough that God would not only take us out to dinner in His Michelin TEN Star Mountaintop Heavenly Restaurant, He would even sacrifice Himself for us.

I can't stop imagining that dinner party though. Looking **at that view** of the other hills and valleys. Looking **at that Throne of God** through the transparent Lapis Lazuli. 'What a great sunset!' you might exclaim as you look around." You might think that this would be a GREAT place to build a church! In fact, they <u>already have</u> built a church there.

Aside from the dinner party, though, imagine He would also give His only Son for us. Jesus **did obey** all of the six hundred thirteen commandments, on our behalf, so that we could live eternally in fellowship with Him. Again, the New Covenant is all about what Jesus did. "For this is how God loved the world. He gave His one and only Son so that everyone who believes in Him will not perish, but have eternal life" (John 3:16 NLT). John 3:17 is often ignored but the message is equally important," God sent His Son into the world not to judge the world, but to save the world through Him." (John 3:17 NLT)

John 3:17 directly contradicts the "Gospel of Condemnation." What idea in our head could stand so strongly against this eternal gift of love? Could it be our feelings of unworthiness conveyed upon us by teachers, pastors, our parents or others when we were growing up?

We can feel entitled to Government benefits, even those we "haven't earned," just because we live in the United States. But we also live today in "The Kingdom of Heaven." That "Parallel

Universes" stuff again…. We feel somehow that we do not deserve the love of God and His Grace and Mercy which offers to receive us as perfect "replicas of His Son." All we need do is acknowledge the truth that God sent His Son (Himself), He died for us (or as us) He was raised, seated with the Father and He wishes us to eternally live with Him in Heavenly Mansions. You do remember, don't you, that Jesus says He is "preparing Heavenly Mansions" for us? "In my Father's House are many mansions; if it were not so, I would have told you. I go to prepare a place for you."(John 14:2 NASB)

God's housing plans for us after we leave this "Vale of Tears" are not just Condos, or small apartments, but in the words of the song they are, "Mansions in the Sky," Don't you get it? Let's prepare to go home with Jesus to our Mansion in the Heavenly Kingdom of God.

Or maybe it's otherwise. Maybe we don't think God is "important enough" to justify our attention. More about that theory in Chapter 9.

God's Grace and Mercy …it's too simple, isn't it? The rewards are too great. Mansions later, blessings and good relationships here and now. Salvation, plus living with and for God should be much more complicated than that, shouldn't it? What could God have possibly had in mind when He made it this simple for us. Why do we feel so unworthy?

Here's a possible explanation. We hear that God is "perfect" and we "know" we are not. As we feel that we are imperfect, somehow we also feel that imperfection is not God's "design error", but our own fault.

Think about it...a perfect being could not possibly have created imperfect beings! That would be like a scientist manufacturing a robot that he knew had design flaws. What scientist would design a robot that would malfunction as soon as the consumer opened the shipping container? Yet, it seems, God did just that.

Lest we misinterpret God's plan, His plan was to "design us to fail under our own power," yet He gave us the ability to choose how to live, where to live and who to serve. He gave us Jesus to redeem us , so that we would be perfect in His sight. Is that what you're saying?" Yep. That's it in a nutshell.

"O.K. then if we are imperfect," you say, "it can't be our fault. It must be someone else's fault! You can say we were designed imperfect by our Creator, but that makes no sense. Wait, I've got it. If we were created perfect - the sin of Adam and all that - then we must have had to continually acknowledge that sin of our forbears and accept our condemnation as inheritors of that 'original sin'. That's it, isn't it? It's all Adam and Eve's fault!"

"Please God, condemn us so we will not have to experience these feelings of imperfection anymore. Lock us up in solitary confinement, so we may meditate on our sins, then kill us." Some Medieval Monks did just that, beating themselves with whips on a daily basis, so their physical pain would perhaps overcome their sense of cosmic unworthiness.

Beating ourselves daily isn't what God wanted. He sent his Son to die for us so that we should **not** feel guilty. Jesus had to die for us so that we and His Dad could live in the same place together. It's past time for us to be thinking like Medieval Monks. It's time for a paradigm shift in our heads.

We're like the adopted child, poor in birth, but taken in by a rich family to live in luxury for the rest of our lives. What did that child do to **earn** the love, or even deserve the love of that adopted family? He **did nothing** but make himself available.

The same is true for us as God's adopted children. He made all of us, to be His children. He intended that we should all receive all the love and blessings He had for us. But, like the Hebrews on Mount Sinai, we do not feel worthy of that personal and intimate love. Some representative like Moses, Billy Graham, our Pastor or Priest should hear God for us. Then he or she could tell us what to do "and we would surely do it."

"Pre-Christians," as Graham Cooke calls anyone who has not yet made a decision for Christ, will often be like the mother desperately cleaning her house before the cleaning lady comes, so that the cleaning lady will not "think less of her." If we did not clean first, the cleaning lady would doubtless, gossip to our neighbors about "what a disaster their house is." There must be a "standard" to which we have to conform as human beings, to be ready for God's Love. I often tell "Pre-Christians" that "Jesus never cleaned a fish before He caught it."

What a surprise to God we must have been! We were caught up in sin and evil doing like the "miserable wretches we are"! But not to God; that's not God's point of view. He created us imperfect. God gave us a mind and a spirit. God gave us free-will and choice, which He knew, that in our own strength, would lead to our downfall.

That's why God had a Savior in mind for us since the day of Creation! He knew we would need one. He gave us one, no strings attached. Just believe the "Gospel of Jesus" and you can join in God's Heavenly Kingdom here on Earth and live with Him forever in His Heavenly Kingdom.

As Jesus said to the thief on the cross, "Truly I say to you, today you will be with Me in Paradise!"(Luke 23:43 ESV) Why did Jesus say that? Was it because the thief had a great testimony? Was it all the good deeds the thief had done? Not then, he was dying on a cross for crimes, even he admitted he had committed. Was it because he had been baptized as a child? We don't know.

As far as the Bible tells us, the thief on the cross next to Jesus was simply a condemned criminal receiving the punishment he deserved. Jesus, saw that the thief defended Him to his companion on the other "thief cross."The other thief mocked Jesus. But when Jesus heard the one testify that he believed that Jesus had committed no sin, and wanted to "be remembered by you when you come into your Kingdom." That's when Jesus affirmed, "You're with me. We're going to be in Paradise together." The past no longer mattered and the thief's future was secure. Just as ours is today, when we too accept that greatest gift.

But before "accept-ions" there must be "expectations." Who do we need to be before God can accept us? What are **our expectations** of who we need to be as "new creatures in Christ" before God will **continue** to eternally welcome us into His home as "the children He has always wanted." How could He possibly welcome us as "the imperfect children we have always been and will probably will still always be," short of a miracle? Well, Virginia, there has been a Miracle! It's the mystery of God living in us so that we may be received and accepted by Him.

I think the "Gospel of Condemnation" has a lot to do with "who we have been told that we should <u>think</u> we are and what we <u>should think</u> we deserve." That is a complex and somewhat convoluted thought. In short, our identity has to do with our who God thinks we are, not who we or other people think we are. As we take on God's thoughts about us from the Bible, we create our own thoughts about "our identity." Where are those negative thoughts coming from? Not from the Word of God.

In our minds, it's all on us. It's all on what we have to do to "make up for" who we've been. He created us. He knew how we would turn out, left to wallow in our own choices. Is He surprised? Is He disappointed? Maybe, but <u>personally I would be surprised</u> if the "omniscient omnipresent and wise creator of the Universe was ever surprised by anything.

God doesn't have high expectations for us. Did God intend for us to wallow in self-pity? Did He intend for us to serve Him in chains as a formerly rebellious slave Did He intend for us to beat ourselves like the Medieval Monks No, as with the Israelites in Egypt, He did not intended to rescue us from slavery into a self dependent life without Him. He delivered us so we would turn to His Son, Jesus, and receive the greatest gift of all. He intended for us to find our true identity, not as slaves, but as Priests in the Kingdom of God.

At Christmas, we celebrate God's Birth as a man. He was given to us to live in us. "God in us", Immanuel, is the greatest gift we could ever receive. But for most of us, that's not the type of Christmas we have been raised to expect.

Like Eating Jelly With Chop Sticks

Jack Narvel

Chapter 8

Christmas Expectations – How Do We Disappoint Ourselves?

Christmas … The most wonderful time of the year! But if that is so, why do we see so many people depressed at Christmas? I think it comes from disappointment.

I looked up "disappointment" in Merriam and Webster's Dictionary. Those two guys apparently agreed to define "disappointment" as the "failure to meet an expectation or hope."

With that definition in mind has God ever failed to meet your expectations? You had your fine hopes and dreams but God DIDN'T seem to be on board with that? You felt He disappointed you, didn't you? Have you "put your trust in Him," only to have something happen, which you feel (NO, you <u>know</u>) had to be less than God's best for you?

I put my "Trust in God," as it says we all should on the back of our U.S. Dollar bill.("In God We Trust") Yet I have been disappointed. While risking being condemned for apostasy, I must confess I have felt that way. "Father forgive me for I have sinned. I confess I have been disappointed at Christmas. Yes, even at this "most wonderful time of the year."

When I was working with psychologists to help people conquer "psychosomatic illness" through using "Biofeedback" instruments, I was surprised to find that when "Think of Christmas" was mentioned as a stimulus to the subject universally, the readings of higher stress would be displayed on the electronic instruments. On the other hand, asking them to think of an image of a Sunday afternoon drive on a country road in Autumn weather always brought on a physiological response of relaxation.

After many trials, and meditations, it finally occurred to me that Christmas was stressful because of our unmet expectations, which often "draw to a head" at that time. When you recall the lyrics of the "Christmas Song": "Chestnuts Roasting on an Open Fire," it tells us that, "kids from one to ninety-two" are wired to expect more from the Christmas Holiday than it can ever possibly deliver. Disappointment at Christmas for most people is a given.

Now Jesus – that's another story, isn't it? How can anyone be disappointed by the man, who is also God, who gave up His life so that we might have life with God the Father and Jesus eternally? The book of Ephesians says that as believers "He made us alive together with Christ. By grace you have been saved, and raised us up with Him and seated in the heavenly places in Christ Jesus." (Ephesians 2:5-6 ESV) "Well," you might say, "that's great for my future in Heaven, but right now on this Earth, I am having some struggles."

If you think our time in the heavenlies with Jesus is all future, not now, I believe you are in error. Let's go back, together, and look, for those of you that think only the King James Version is God's "actual word." Let us look at Ephesians 2:4-8 in the King James Version of the Bible. After all, if that translation was good enough for Paul and Silas, it's good enough for me! Hummph!

Here it is "But God, who is rich in mercy, for His great love wherewith He loved us. Even when we were dead in sins, hath quickened us together with Christ (by grace are you saved); and has raised us up together and made us sit together in the heavenly places in Christ Jesus." (Ephesians 2:4-8 KJV)

Note the tense of the verb "sit" in this passage. It's not "will be seated," it's present tense. Think about it, this means that as believers we both are - in the present - and have been, in the past, seated with Christ since the day we accepted Christ as our savior.

We may not admit or accept the fact, we both "sit" next to Jesus in the Heavenlies (which is a "Parallel Universe" for those of you who are Quantum Physicists) and are simultaneously seated in our chairs here on Earth. That fact is mind-blowing, isn't it? If we are at all conscious of the fact that we live both in the spiritual and the natural, then how can we ever be disappointed?

What about a death over the Holidays? Have you ever personally experienced, or known someone who lost a loved one during the Holidays? Have you heard people say:" Sorry for your loss. I guess the Lord needed him more than we did, so He called him home." WHAT ?!?! God does not need to cause cancer to take someone to be with Him. God miraculously raised Enoch and Elijah into Heaven, without any illness or other bodily harm whatsoever. If God caused illness to "teach his children a lesson," He would be in violation of the laws we have here on Earth to protect our children. God is a much better teacher than that. He is a much better Father than that! He can, and does, teach us about how to live a better life simply though conversations with us and the leading of His Holy Spirit in us.

The enemy takes and steals and kills. God is the giver, the redeemer, and healer. Express your grief, even your anger with God. It's O.K. He can deal with it. He says in Revelation that "I know your works: you are neither cold nor hot. Would that you were either cold or hot! So, because you are lukewarm, and neither hot nor cold, I will spit you out of my mouth." (Revelation 3:15-16 ESV)

Jesus would rather us be "cold or hot" in our emotional state towards Him than "lukewarm." He can handle our emotions. He is only disappointed with us when we appear to "not to give a rip" about Him or His potential influence on our lives. We as humans, on the other hand, are easily disappointed when our expectations fail. Here's an example:

I remember the Christmas of 1955. I had just turned 11 years old. We were having the annual Christmas Eve party at my Uncle Ed's house. I was fortunate indeed to have two "Uncle Eds." One was an attorney and head of the Draft Board on my mother's side (Ed Greenwood) and the other was a steelworker (Ed Irwin), on my father's side. My Father's family gathered Christmas Eve and my mother's family gathered on Christmas Day. Uncle Ed Irwin had a big house. It was out in the country. There was snow on the ground and a big fire in the fireplace. We had a great dinner. Ed had married my father's sister, Emma. Aunt Emma was a great cook! So after eating, we sat around the fireplace looking at the twinkling lights on the Christmas tree and having quiet conversations in the big living room. But then, ...ALL OF A SUDDEN through the front door, in came Cousin Bud Irwin. He was dressed up as Santa (he was the most portly of the relatives) with a floppy cone-shaped red hat with a white pom-pom on top. He came in the front door, without knocking! He had the right to barge in; he was Santa. And with a hearty "Ho, Ho, Ho!" he greeted us all.

Remember those days when relatives would play Santa, with a cheap red suit and an awful fake beard? Clearly, despite the red suit, they had not forsaken their usual identity. No one older than one would have been fooled. To make things even less convincing, "Santa" would take gifts from under the tree rather than from his bag. In fact, he didn't even have a bag.

It was as though the man disguised as Santa was actually a thief who had come to steal our presents from under the tree. But then, as he saw what happy gentle people we were, he changed his mind and decided to pretend to give us what was already ours, the presents instead. This reminds me of how many Christians will beg God to give them what is already theirs: health, wisdom, peace, prosperity. Jesus already died for us, so that we might have all that. More on that subject later But for now, back to Cousin Bud. Perhaps he hoped to avoid a two to five year prison sentence by giving us what was already ours, rather than taking, go figure. Besides, I think our Santa stopped carrying a bag after his first back surgery.

The way this ritual ran in our family was that Santa read a gift tag and handed out the presents. Each time a name was called a child or adult would reach out to receive their gift boxes. The boxes were wrapped in gaily colored paper with a bow. When my name was first called, I did not get a festively wrapped box with a ribbon and bow, but an envelope. Well, O.K., I get it! Someone couldn't think of what to get me, so they gave me money for a gift. That was O.K. once....but it kept going on and on until I had received a gift from each Uncle and Grandma and Grandpa. They were ALL envelopes.

I was nearly in tears. I didn't know exactly why at that time. I realize, now, that I must have thought the cash meant "no one cared enough for me to shop for a gift I would like." We were a close-knit family that got together several times a year, yet no one felt they knew me well enough to buy a gift for me that I would like. Maybe it was "too much trouble" to take the time out of their busy schedules to go to the store, or shop the mail order catalogs, to buy me a gift I would have liked. So they gave me money instead…. I was deeply disappointed. Even a tie in a wrapped box would have been better than an envelope.

My uncle Charlie saw the upset on my face and came over to me: "What's wrong, Jackie." Charlie may not have known me well enough to get me a gift I would have liked, but he knew me well enough to tell I was distressed. Charlie was my favorite Uncle because he had a great sense of humor. He laughed a lot and tended to make light of things. But on this occasion, he did not try to make light of my predicament.

I said, almost in tears: "Uncle Charlie, no one got me a present!" "Well, that's not true, Jackie, we all gave you presents," he said.

"But Uncle Charlie, (I'm eleven years old, then) I didn't want money. I was hoping for a board game or a card game or something like that." Charlie said, "Well, but Jackie, you can use the money to buy whatever you like."

"It's still not the same," I said.

Imagine the scene if you will. Christmas Eve and all the adults and other kids are tearing the wrapping paper from their gifts. The floor is piling high with colorful paper, which is then thrown into the fireplace like an offering to Pelé!

With a bunch of envelopes in my hand, I felt completely different. I was like a handicapped person in a room full of marathon runners. I had been singled out by God to be totally embarrassed and frustrated in front of my Father's family. But wait, my uncle Charlie was moved to action! He spoke quietly to Uncle Ed and explained the situation. Then Ed said, "Well, Jackie I'd like to give you a game. We have a bunch up here in the closet." Would you like to pick one?"

So I pointed to one, but now I was not only disappointed I was also embarrassed. Many of the family had noticed something was wrong, and that "little Jackie" was the cause of it! I thought they were all watching me, I was not only different; I was obviously ungrateful. Wretch that I was! We were a family of Methodists and Presbyterians and former Catholics. We didn't do well with expressions of emotion, particularly at family gatherings. And emotions that involved tears …well those emotions might not be satiated by anything deeper than a kiss on the cheek and accompanied by a short lived one-armed hug.

I'm disappointed, I'm embarrassed, BUT NOW, I MUST take a game from the closet, otherwise, Uncles Ed and Charlie would be disappointed too. Imagine the trauma for the family. Here is a glorious time of the year when we celebrate our Savior's Birth but people are disappointed and crying at the family Christmas Party. These are emotions that should be reserved for Maundy Thursday, not Christmas.

Of course, being a good and thoughtful son to my father and not wishing to cause further upset to his family. I took down a game and pretended it was just what I had wanted. I have no remembrance today of what game it might have been. Maybe "Clue." The irony to my mind at the time would have been: "What a perfect gift, the relatives hadn't a "Clue" of what to give me."

All in all, my disappointment that year caused probably my worst Christmas Eve, ever. But, as I faded into unconsciousness in bed that night, I could dream and look forward to my Uncle Ed Greenwood's annual Christmas Day party. My mother's family was great. They were all doctors and lawyers. They all had lots of money and a gorgeous house on top of the Hill overlooking the City of Coatesville. The cousins were more sociable. I may not have been a selfish kid, but I did understand the significance of "the butter and the bread."Ungrateful wretch that I was.

Christmas Day more than made up for Christmas Eve. My uncle's Cocker Spaniel came to me to lick my hands and face. I had other young cousins to play with. AND we had another great Christmas Dinner. But finally, oh yes…NO ONE GAVE ANYONE MONEY. Funny isn't it how to those who have money, money is not an appropriate gift. But if you don't have much money, then you are probably looking to have more money. To you, then money would seem like the "perfect gift." Maybe not so much to pre-teenage kids. Go figure… but on Christmas Day, at my Uncle Ed Greenwood's house, I got toys and games!

As one expectation and hope were dashed on Christmas Eve, a place was created for my heart to be filled on Christmas Day. You may think I was being selfish, and what's the lesson in that? Well, O.K. then; you got it! But I will exclaim: "What an AWESOME God we serve!"

Now that I've told my story of selfish disappointment, you may be asking: "Well, Jack I know God has got my back and in time, he can turn the bad to good, but just to be on the safe side, is there a way I can I avoid those disappointments in life?" Should we just turn off our brains and never ask for anything? Never desire anything? Do I become a Buddhist and seek Nirvana rather than stuff?" Good questions! But, if you are already a believer in Christ, that Buddhist thing probably wouldn't work for you.

Instead, let's look in the Bible. You remember there were these three guys who set themselves up NOT to be disappointed in the face of adversity. How did they do that? Is there a lesson for us today which we can learn from their behavior?

As you may recall from the book of Daniel: Shadrach, Meshach, and Abednego were about to be cast into the fiery furnace by King Nebuchadnezzar unless they would deny the God of Israel, and worship the towering gold statue of the King instead. They said a very memorable thing:

"Shadrach, Meshach, and Abednego replied, 'O Nebuchadnezzar, we are not worried about what will happen to us. If we are thrown into the flaming furnace, our God is able to deliver us; and he will deliver us out of your hand, Your Majesty. But if he doesn't, please understand, sir, that even then we will never, under any circumstance, serve your gods or worship the gold statue you have erected.'"(Daniel 3:16-20 TLB)

With this statement, the three Hebrew transplants in Babylon guaranteed they would never be disappointed with God. If they survive the fire, great, "Praise the Lord!" If they are killed in the fire, also great, because they knew deep in their hearts that they would be translated from the furnace into Heaven. They would be totally trusting, thankful and grace-filled regardless of the outcome of their circumstances. Great attitude, isn't it?

A passage in Hebrews says: "Now faith is the substance of things hoped for, the evidence of things not seen. For by it the elders obtained a good testimony. By faith, we understand that the worlds were framed by the word of God so that the things which are seen were not made of things which are visible." (Hebrews 11:1-3 NLT)

This passage actually describes what science has proven today through "Quantum Physics." Subatomic particles (the unseen) can be influenced by our thoughts and observations. With our faith and belief, we are capable of doing just what God did, to create something out of nothing, or at least what appears to be nothing.

Think about it. That's what an artist does with a canvas. That's what an inventor does with an invention. We are told in the bible that as believers we all have "the mind of Christ" and Jesus even told the disciples, "Truly, truly, I say to you whoever believes in Me will also do the works that I do; and greater works than these will he do, because I am going to the Father."(John 14:12 ESV)

We have been given amazing power as believers and disciples of Christ today, yet we still struggle with disappointment. We still think we are unworthy. Why on Earth, or Heaven for that matter, would that be?

What is it then, that we can "hope for" without expectations that may be crushed? When God created the Universe out of invisible things, He knew that in speaking the world into existence, it would surely form, just as He intended. He simply said,"Earth Be!" and it was. It formed just as He imagined it would! I'll bet God didn't think, even for a microsecond,"I wonder what I'll do if it doesn't form like I was expecting." God does not doubt as we often do.

The undeniable hope that we have at Christmas is shown by The Father Himself. Christmas is a season of hope and faith.

We can see the lights and the store displays, but much in the spiritual remains unseen. "Great, I believe that God created the 'seen out of the unseen,'" you say, "but what about this Christmas disappointment thing? How can I do what those three guys did in the furnace?" Great question again. It has to do with what you are expecting, and something called "belief."

A song in Psalms says "One thing have I desired of the Lord, that will I seek after; that I may dwell in the House of the LORD, all the days of my life. To behold the beauty of the LORD, and to enquire in His temple." (Psalms27:4 KJV) Can that hope ever be defeated?

Think about it, Christmas is traditionally a season where we focus on the concept that "it is better to give than receive." We are taught at church and probably at school to let our own concerns be downplayed for a few weeks while we expand our horizons to encompass the needs of others. Why not? Hey, it's only once a year… let's get with the program. Put some quarters, or even a dollar bill or two in that bucket that the Salvation Army Bell Ringer has in front of Walmart. But, (God Forbid) remember folks, we didn't come to the store to "give" we came to "get." We came to get something for someone else or even ourselves. Didn't we?

In the next chapter, we'll look at the Apostle Peter's disappointment with God. Not at Christmas, but at the Mount of Olives, at Passover. Oh my Lord! It was a time of celebration in remembrance of God's love in freeing the Israelites from their slavery in Egypt. How embarrassing to misapprehend God at a time like that, but Peter did.

Like Eating Jelly With Chop Sticks   Jack Narvel

Chapter 9

Disappointment with God – Who is He Really?

I have always admired Peter in the Bible stories. He was a rough uneducated fisherman. He was trained by his Earthly father for a single purpose. Bring home food and money through fishing, "just like our family has always done." Yet somehow, what was inside of Peter was apparent to Jesus, even when He had first seen him. Something to do with Jesus being God and God being omniscient, I think. But when Peter was chosen by Jesus, he contended he was unworthy. He apparently felt like Isaiah, he was a "man of unclean lips" and other "unacceptable stuff." But, Jesus insisted Peter join Him anyway, despite Peter's doubts.

The tables soon turned. Once Peter was a part of the twelve disciples, he walked with them and attended Jesus "training meetings." After some of this intimacy with The LORD, Peter began to have expectations of Jesus. Peter thought surely this excellent teacher is also the Messiah, predicted by Jewish scriptures, who would become a King on Earth. Surely Jesus would maintain his "council of twelve" and Peter would be elevated to rich and honored status in Jesus' Kingdom of Heaven on Earth.

At the last Supper when all the disciples were present, Peter assured Jesus that even if everyone else ran away, Peter would never leave Him. Of course, Peter did not see the immediate future. He was imagining a "Royal Court" of which he was to be a significant part. Shortly after dinner was over, his hopes were crushed when Jesus was taken away by the Temple guards.

Peter was a fighter! He would fight John and James to decide who got to sit next to Jesus in His throne room. He did this right in front of Jesus! He was surely capable of squelching this attack on Jesus by wielding his sword and cutting off the guards ear. "What next, Jesus?" "Let's gut these Temple guards like fish! Lord, I'll defend you!" Peter is so tough and capable, it is not beyond his imagination that he will defend even God Himself from human attack!

If you'll remember from the stories of Jesus and His disciples in the first four books of the New Testament. Peter was always the "out of control" guy. Peter was irrepressible. When Jesus asked, "But who do you say I am?" Peter was the guy who responded immediately, "You are the Christ, the Son of the living God!" (Matt 16:15-16.ESV). Then Jesus responded, "Blessed are you, Simon Bar-Jonah! For flesh and blood has not revealed this to you, but my Father who is in heaven."(Matt 16:17 ESV)

GOOD JOB, PETER! Nothing like getting a huge compliment from the boss. Peter must have had a huge smile. He must have been rubbing his hands together with joy! But then Jesus tells the disciples not to tell anyone that He is the Messiah. And, Jesus is not yet done with Peter. Jesus gives Peter what the Roman Catholic Church has assumed to be Peter's identity in Christ: "And I tell you, you are Peter "the Rock(or stone)," (no longer Simon "he has heard") and on this rock, I will build my church, and the gates of hell shall not prevail against it." (Matt 16:18 ESV)

Most Non-Catholic commentaries would say that in changing Simon's name to Peter, it was simply a change Jesus declared out of respect for this untrained fisherman's ability to hear the voice of God. The "rock "on which Jesus would build his church was the Faith and belief of Peter, not the human being Peter himself. Later in Matthew 16:21, Jesus tells the disciples how He must suffer and die. Peter, the recently declared "Rock," "Took Him aside and began to rebuke Him, privately. 'Never,Lord!' he said. 'This shall never happen to you!'"(Matt 16:22 NLT)

Jesus is the Messiah, Peter had recently declared that. Yet now he chooses to argue with the Messiah, as though they both came from the same World View. But, as we know today, they did not.

Jesus responds: "Out of my way, Satan! You stand right in my path, Peter, when you look at things from man's point of view and not from God's" (Matt 16:23 J. B. Phillips). Despite his recent name change, Peter had no idea who Jesus really was or who Peter was. Apparently Peter had stopped "being the one who hears," (God) to the one who was listening to the leading of his own "soulishness (your mind, will, and emotions)."

But at the Sea of Galilee, Peter was finally convinced by The Spirit of God that Jesus is the "real deal." Jesus had been resurrected from the dead! Peter saw the empty tomb. WOW! Then Jesus tells him personally what Peter's calling is: "Feed my Lambs."(John 21:15 KJV)

Peter's expectations of Jesus and his desire to protect Him, were inspired by Peter's own desires to be elevated from "humble fisherman" to "honored member of Jesus' Earthly court."

Peter tried to dictate how the Christ should behave. How about us? Peter thought he had God boxed in just right as Peter's "eternal Christmas present." How have we boxed in God?

Peter had walked with God for three years. Many of us have been saved for 20 or more years. We've seen miracles in our own lives, maybe not like the ones Peter personally witnessed, but miracles none-the-less. God's "playbook" is beyond our human reasoning. It wasn't written the way Peter, or perhaps we today, expected.

In fact, Jesus Himself never acted independently. Jesus says He could not do "anything which He wanted."Jesus said, "Truly, truly, I say to you, the Son can do nothing of His own accord, but only what He sees the Father doing. For whatever the Father does, that the Son does likewise." (John 5:19 ESV)

So unlike Peter, Jesus had cast aside His pride long ago. He knows He is God, He also knows he is fully human. Unlike most of us, Jesus knew He could do things beyond "human capability," (Miracles) in His Father's power. Yet He choses to limit Himself for our benefit. Jesus wants us to see that we, too, can have a personal relationship with God the Father, just as He did. We too can accomplish miracles through our belief and acceptance of Him as our Savior and Redeemer. Back in Matthew 16 Jesus says: "Anyone who intends to come with me, has to let me lead. You're not in the driver's seat – I am. Don't run from suffering, embrace it. Follow Me and I'll show you how. … What good is it to get everything you want and lose yourself, the real you?" That's a great message for Christmas right there. Don't seek stuff for yourself or even for your family, but seek Jesus with all your heart and soul."(Matt 16:24 MSG) "Seek ye first the Kingdom of God, and His righteousness; and all these things shall be added unto you."(Matt 6:33 KJV)

Peter expected Jesus to be an Earthly King. But as Jesus said to Pilate: "My Kingdom is not of this world. If My Kingdom were of this world, my servants would have been fighting, that I might not be delivered over to the Jews. But my Kingdom is not of this world."(John 18:36 ESV)

Peter tried to save Jesus from the Temple Guards– but it wasn't necessary. In fact, In order for prophecy to be fulfilled, Jesus had to be handed over to the Romans to be crucified so that through His death and ressurection all humanity might be redeemed.

According to the Book of Revelation, Jesus will one day be the actual ruling King of the earth: "And He will rule them with a rod of iron." (Revelation 2:27 ESV) But not in Pilate's day and certainly not today. Yes, today we are living in the Kingdom of God. BUT we can't see it in the physical. Looks to me like "All Hell is breaking loose!" How about you?

Why doesn't God act sooner? Why doesn't He fulfill our expectations of an all-powerful, loving and just God? The answer is simple, because: in Genesis man was given that power"And God blessed them (Adam and Eve) and said to them, "Be fruitful and multiply and fill the Earth and subdue it, and have dominion … over every living thing that moves on the earth." (Genesis 1:28 ESV)

When we are expecting God to act on our behalf, it is rather we who need to believe and make it so. Mankind was set up as the ruler of this world. Everything on earth was subjugated to Him. God transferred His power and authority to us, as regards earthly matters.

As Jesus did for Peter, He will also do for us. We are under a New Covenant where Jesus is our high priest and mediator. He says at the cross, all things that scripture had promised are now fulfilled. "It is finished" (John 19:28-30 NKJV) and in Isaiah 43:25 and Hebrews 8:12 that he will not only forgive (blot out) our sins, but He will "remember our sins no more." So no need for guilt or shame at Christmas! Jesus has forgiven and forgotten our sins. Why shouldn't we do the same?

I posted a sermon from Bill Johnson of Bethel Church, on Facebook once. The sermon was about how we need to forgive ourselves. I had to take the post down because it created so much anger and correction. "How can we forgive ourselves?" said one post "Only Jesus can forgive sins." O.K. great point, but then who lives in us? Jesus. Can the Jesus who lives in us forgive our sins and create in us a heart that "remembers those sins no more?" I believe he can.

Getting back to the expectations of Christmas in Chapter 8, what is your expectation of God at Christmas? Will God get you the winning Lotto Ticket? Maybe … Maybe not. Will He heal your wounded soul? Absolutely… but you will have to allow Him to do so. He always gives us a freewill choice.

Peter the fisherman was a swaggering uneducated, selfish braggart, but when he was full of the Holy Spirit he led over three thousand souls to The Lord at Pentecost.

At Pentecost, Peter submitted himself to the leading of the Holy Spirit, as The Lord asks us to do today. No more expectations of God doing what we want. Only the expectation that as the Holy Spirit leads us, so He will equip us.

As Americans living in contentious times, in 2019, (depending on our political affiliation) God has not called us to curse the staff of CNN, to curse Nancy Pelosi, nor to curse Donald Trump or Ilhan Omar. Rather, He has called us to "Hold fast the confession of our hope without wavering, for He who promised is faithful. And let us consider how to stir up one another to love and good works, not neglecting to meet together as is the habit of some, but encouraging one another, and all the more as you see the day (of His return) drawing near." (Hebrews 10:23-25 ESV). As Christians on Earth, even at this troublesome and conflicted time, we are called by God to Bless others, with our words and deeds, not to curse them.

At Christmas, and even the rest of our lives, let's remember that it's not all about us. It's not about how much or what we get. It's not how often we fast or pray or read the word. It's not about volunteering for church projects (but please feel welcome to do so, especially if you go to my church). It's about a relationship with Jesus and trusting in Him for everything in our lives. Every day, even every moment, we are seeking Him, rather than self-fulfillment. We do this certainly not under our own power, but His. AND we give Him all the Glory!

"Trust in the Lord, and do a good deed. Settle down and keep company with God. Open up before God. Hold nothing back and He'll do whatever needs to be done. Dwell in the Land and befriend faithfulness with all your heart mind and soul and God will give you the desires of your heart." (Psalm 37:3 MSG) Why is that? Because He put those desires in our hearts in the first place. Fulfilling the desires He put there is just the manifestation of the real deal.

Remember King Solomon? When God told him to "ask for anything, and I will give it to you?" Solomon asked for wisdom. Did God disappoint him? No. "Then God said to him: 'Because you have asked this thing, and have not asked long life for yourself, nor have you asked riches for yourself, nor have asked for the life of your enemies, but have asked for yourself understanding to discern justice, behold, I have done according to your words; see I have given you a wise and understanding heart, so that there has never been anyone like you before you, nor will there ever be. Moreover, I will give you what you have not asked for - both wealth and honor, so that in your lifetime you will have no equal among kings." (1Kings 3:11-13.NIV)

God said because Solomon asked for wisdom and not wealth and fame, God gave him wisdom and all the physical stuff that goes with it. Pretty nice gift. Suddenly it was all Solomon's.

When we pray to God, hopefully, we're not always asking Him for "stuff." Ideally, prayer is a conversation between friends. It is O.K. to ask Him for something in the midst of those conversations. What are you asking for this year? If you are asking humbly in deference to God, you just might get what you asked for and some "suddenlies" as well.

Who are we in Christ? We are the "sons and daughters of the Most High God." If that is true then how shall we act? What shall we expect? There are some clues in the next chapters.

Like Eating Jelly With Chop Sticks			Jack Narvel

Like Eating Jelly With Chop Sticks   Jack Narvel

Chapter 10

When God Just Isn't Good Enough

In previous chapters we've seen people experience faith challenging hardships, like 9/11 and the Duckboat Tragedy on Table Lake in the Ozarks. We've seen the disappointments of myself and others when life just doesn't seem to treat us as we'd like. We've read about how Peter, Jesus' disciple for three years, totally misread Jesus and His mission on Earth. Jesus, the man Peter thought would be an Earthly King and live a long time on Earth (with Peter at His side) was suddenly taken from him.

Can people's Faith survive this level of disappointment? Is God like a bad waiter at a restaurant who screws up the serving of your dinner, and spills the drinks in your lap? Is God like a bad cook, who burns the Chicken and sends it out anyway? If you had an experience like that, you might well say, "We'll never go back to that restaurant again!"

Many people DO see God that way, don't they? Worse, they confuse God with the Pastor. When people are not appreciated the way they thought they should be, then it's time to change churches. Congregants, even those who have been part of Church leadership, get disappointed with the Pastor and throw him out. Sometimes, they even throw him out without notice. I was part of a church that engaged a new Pastor while the existing one was on vacation. He returned to find his personal things boxed up and ready to go. There was a new man at his old desk.

In other cases, members of the Church, will get "fed up" with their Pastor and his teachings or his attitude and seek another Church, more supportive of their own theology, or more supportive of "who they think they are." They may even start their own churches. Sometimes those become the "Church of the Glorification of Self." It's not always that way. But it happens. Psychology tells us that, "The Ego" is "who we think we are." The Holy Spirit tells us "who God thinks we are." Which is the more correct?

Do these people seeking God in a Pastor, or seeking the glorification of themselves in a church, ever find true peace? Do they find the ultimate meaning for their lives by skipping from place to place, or going from Pastor to Pastor in their existing place?

It may be true for some, but in my experience, it is seldom the case. Rather than seeking to serve, they are seeking the best place to be served. Like those regulars at Sam Wo's Chinese restaurant, they may feel most comfortable in a setting where the Pastor "sends them to Hell" every week, rather than sharing Gods unending, forgiving and passionate love. As we have seen earlier, the popularity of The Gospel of Condemnation seems to fit well with the negative expectancies of many believers.

And how about the Pastors themselves? I am aware of at least two in my personal experience who were simply not suited for the ministry. They got into it because father, grandfather, or other relatives had been in it. Ministry was like a "Family Business" to which you were "naturally attracted" and in which a spot for you would be held until you were ready.

The problem in these cases is that both God and his congregation have disappointed the Pastor. The governing board is happy with him because he can engagingly tell Bible stories. The people, who come to these services, are entertained by the choir and the stories but are never challenged to know the true character of God. They never even glimpse "God as He really is." There is no dinner on Mount Sinai for them, not even in their dreams. They reject the concept of getting to know the Christ in themselves. As these misdirected pastors and their misdirected congregations are led by the Holy Spirit to change their hearts and minds, they may find the truth of God, imparted by the Holy Spirit in their souls. But, they need to be listening for it, otherwise, that change of heart will pass them by.

By misapprehending God, many of us miss the true emancipation from emotional slavery to Earthly concerns. We miss the freedom that the manifestation of our faith can bring. As Henry David Thoreau once wrote:"The mass of men lead lives of quiet desperation. What is called 'resignation' (to one's circumstances) is (really) confirmed desperation. From the desperate city, you go into the desperate country and have to console yourself with the bravery of minks and muskrats. A stereotyped, but unconscious despair is concealed even under what are called the games and amusements of mankind. There is no 'play' in them, for (real play) comes after work. "(On Walden Pond, orig. pub. date, 1845)

I was taken by this quote from Thoreau when I read "On Walden Pond" in High School. It resonated with my soul at that time and still does. The simple life, removed from daily obligations to work or to have interactions with others, can be its own reward. We can so easily fall into despair, and then chronic depression as we see our expectations, however "unreasonable," dashed to death by how we perceive reality treating us.

No well-intended consolation by friend, relative, priest, pastor or Doctor of Psychiatry can successfully battle our own underlying belief about ourselves, or how we see others. Not without our willingness to see the true Gospel of Christ embodied in us. As Paul writes: "Be not conformed to this world but renew your mind with the washing of the Word."(Romans 12:2 KJV)

I like the Message Translation of Romans 12:1-2. I think it summarizes this issue even more clearly: "Here's what I want you to do, God helping you, take your everyday ordinary life, your sleeping, eating, going to work and walking around life, place it before God as an offering. Embracing what God does for you is the best thing you can do for Him. Don't become so well adjusted to your culture that you fit into it without even thinking. Instead, fix your attention on God, you'll be changed from the inside out. Readily recognize what He wants from you and quickly respond to it. Unlike the culture around you, always dragging you down to its level of immaturity, God brings the best out of you, develops well-formed maturity in you." (Romans 12:1-2 MSG)

If changing churches doesn't seem to "do the trick for you," if changing Pastors doesn't do it, then maybe, just maybe, changing your point of view about God, and who you are in Him, might be worth a try. The two pastors who came to mind in my previous example changed their life's work, after many frustrating years in Church ministry. Both became social workers because counseling and encouragement was the part of ministry they always found most rewarding.

As pastors, we often end up preaching to ourselves, getting more out of the message that God gives us than some in the congregation may get. Another benefit of being a Pastor is that we avoid the embarrassment of snoring in church. It's hard to fall asleep when you're standing behind the podium.

The things that challenge our faith most are always those areas of self-doubt, which are caused by an inaccurate perception of who God is for us and in us. By the misapprehension of who God is in us, we will also miss the truth of who we are. The most common fallacy that we tend to embrace is that our Heavenly Father is like our earthly father. That can of worms, when opened, can lead to years of frustration and despair, depending, of course on your experience of your earthly father.

When I was first "saved," (or scared into believing God was a punisher of men who acted outside of His desires for us), I was thirteen years of age. I had come to this summer Bible camp on a beautiful lake to have fun with my friends from Church. Instead, on the first night there, I heard the evangelist's words of condemnation: "You are worse than the Roman soldier who threw a spear into the side of our Lord, as he hung helplessly on the Cross, if you will not accept this great salvation which the Lord is offering you today!"

I was scared out of my wits by this revelation of an angry God who was ready to kill me if I didn't swear to love Him. Some friends have told me that the women in their lives are sometimes that way. "Don't cross them, or they will kill you! Tell them you love them, no matter what! Be safe, not sorry!" I had to believe the Evangelist's words to be accurate because they sounded so much like what my earthly father would say to me.

The worst, experience I had of the conditional love from my earthly father, was this incident: After I confessed to taking a Reader's Digest magazine from the College library, my father said: "What have I raised: a thief? Why can't you be more like your nice friend, Tommy?"

Ah yes, truly it is said: "comparison is the thief of joy."

I was ready to kill my father and myself at that moment. I felt that I couldn't live any longer with his conditional love. I aimed my 1962 Volkswagen Beetle at a nearby telephone pole and said: "If you don't apologize and take that back, I'm driving us into that telephone pole." My roommate was in the back seat and later told me he was praying for my father to "take the hint." He knew I was serious and so did my father. My father quickly said: "I'm sorry; please forgive me." I steered the car back onto the road.

At that point in my life, I had decided that my days of "quiet desperation" were over. By ending it all, there and then, I would perhaps be in a better place. Frankly, I was not thinking that suicide might be seen as "the Unforgivable Sin" that might confine me to the fires of Hell for eternity. But, in my seventeen-year-old mind, the fires of Hell could not be any worse than the condemnation I felt from my Earthly father at that moment.

It has recently been released, in psychological studies, that the mass killings in High Schools had almost universally been motivated by the killer's response to rejection by his peers.

There are times when, if we were to admit it, we would like to kill this judgmental and disapproving God, whose love we had so desperately desired, but whose love had turned out to be conditional. We felt rejected by the Supreme Being whom we were told was the embodiment of pure love. We found we could no longer meet the conditions of His pleasure and therefore, life was no longer worth living. Under those circumstances we would like to kill God and kill ourselves at the same time. I suspect, that in the case of some suicides, that was exactly what was on their minds. We may feel we need to end it all because of the lack of love from God, or men or women. <u>If love is always conditional, then it's natural for us to become desperate in constantly trying to earn it.</u>

In the extension of that scenario, I am standing at the Heavenly Gates, in front of St. Peter, who is poring over "The Lamb's Book of Life" to see if my name was still written there, or had it been "blotted out?"…I would say: "I'm sorry Pete, but life was just all too much. I never got the love I desired from either men, women or God, so I just did what I thought I had to do to make it all jibe with my belief system." (No response from Peter, he is still paging through the book). "By the way," I say, "is God still dead? I know Nietzsche thought he had killed God, but God seemed to bounce back from that one." Still, no response from Pete. I say," So wazzup, Pete, can I come in, or do I have to go to 'The Other Place'? I'm sorry I took my own life, Pete, I really am, but I just felt like I had no other choice."

These thoughts are clearly the musings of a deranged mind. Or are they more commonly held than I might think? As believers, under God's Grace, we should never doubt that Heaven is open to us regardless of our behavior. I have talked to many people who doubt that Heaven is open to them, even after being "saved." When asked if they are going to Heaven when they die, I've heard some believers say,"I hope so." Then we go through the questions:"Do you believe that Jesus is the son of God? (yes) do you believe He died for your sins (yes) do you believe that He sits at the right hand of God interceding for you (yes) have you given your heart and your life to The Lord (yes) Then are you going to Heaven when you die? "I sure hope so."... I can imagine God's frustration with us, at times like this...

If you aren't "saved from Hell" what are you being saved from? If you aren't going to Heaven, where do you think you are going when you "slough off this mortal coil?"

Is unredeemed humanity doomed to a life of dashed expectations and eternal disappointments or is it simply a matter of changing our hearts and minds and going to a better restaurant. Perhaps we are all looking for a place without condemning waiters and a condemning God.

Do we really have that choice in life, or is it apostasy even to think like that? I don't think so. I believe the apostasy comes from harboring and encouraging the belief within ourselves that - <u>contrary to the teachings about God in the Bible</u> - <u>God is an angry and judgmental God.</u>

Our friends, Merriam and Webster in their Dictionary say they think "apostasy' is "an act of refusing to continue to follow, obey or recognize a religious faith." I know many who have come to the true understanding of "the Gospel of Grace," who would certainly fit that definition. They have found the truth of the Gospel and have left the Pastors and Churches which condemned them to Hell every week. But does that "apostasy" make them "evil"?

Many of us were brought up in Religion to think that His "Grace" can happen only once. Grace happens when we first confess our sins and allow that He is our personal Lord and Savior. After that moment, any missing of God's ultimate, or even momentary, desire for our lives will result in eternal condemnation.

To avoid that condemnation, we must go to our priest, pastor, or marriage counselor, praying fervently with them asking, like King David,"Have mercy on me O God, according to your steadfast love; according to your abundant mercy blot out my transgressions. Wash me thoroughly from my iniquity and cleanse me from my sin."(Ps 51:1-2 ESV)

We beg forgiveness confessing our shortcomings on a weekly (if we were Roman Catholic) or even daily basis, promising to do better (or at least differently) next time. "Whew! Dodged that bullet, but just barely." Isn't that what Religions teach us?

But as I've noted in this book before, the Bible tells us in the Old Testament (Isaiah 43:25) and in the New Testament (Hebrews 8:12), that God will "blot out our transgressions for My Own Sake, and remember them no more." Interesting isn't it that the language here is "for my own sake"…not because we have used the right language in speaking to God to apologize or confess our shortcomings, but "for His own sake."

Like an exceptional Earthly father, who loves us unconditionally all the time, even when we have taken his most valuable possession and wrecked it, (our hearts) our Heavenly Father forgives us and continues to seek to restore our hearts. This Heavenly seeking of our hearts even continues when we reject His Son whom He sent to redeem us.

The unforgivable sin as described in Mark 3:28-29, in Matthew 12:31 and Luke 12:10 is "Blasphemy against the Holy Spirit." According to *dictionary.com*: "Blasphemy is any statement that construes that God is unkind, unjust or cruel." Another interesting definition is in Merriam and Webster's Dictionary. They say,"Blasphemy shares a root with 'blame'. Both words may be traced to the Greek 'blasphemein' or to speak ill of."

Therefore, one wonders if those preachers who tell us that God is a "condemning God," rather than a "loving God" are the true "blasphemers?" More on that later.

So how does definition of blasphemy fit with "The Gospel of Condemnation"? Some would think it fits perfectly because it implies, if not said openly, that God is "just" but cruel in His justice. He is the Judge isn't He? He is bound by Law, isn't He? Like the Roman soldier beating Jesus on the whipping post, God would exact on us at least the 40 lashes allowed by law. Why not, after all, we were disobedient!

Tough Call, not just for lay-persons, but for Pastors, Priests, and Doctors of all sorts. How can God be a God of Justice and a God of Mercy and Compassion all at the same time?

Are we back to the concept to "Parallel Universes" where God can not only be in two places at once (we NEVER did question that one) but can He be two different entities at once? Two different personalities at once? One hateful and One loving? This discussion has vexed theologians and accounted for splits in the Church.

Checking the Old Testament (where surely God's desire for Justice outweighs his Mercy) we find that God, in the book of Jonah, strongly disapproves of the Ninevites behavior. They are persecuting his children Israel. So Jonah is directed by God to go to Nineveh, under his own great protest, to tell the Ninevites that the God of Israel has doomed them for their behavior. Naturally they accept this message as truth. Would't you? Here's a guy draped in seaweed and fish entrails, smelling like last week's garbage saying,"I have a word from God for you!" On second thought, maybe not. BUT, after they repent and put on sackcloth and ashes, God forgives them and restores their Nation.

Jonah takes that opportunity to explain to God why he didn't want to come to Nineveh in the first place. "You are a merciful and compassionate God, slow to get angry and abiding filled with unfailing love. You are eager to turn back from destroying people." (Jonah 4:2 NLT)

Jonah hates the Ninevites, but in his heart of hearts, he knew that God would relent from His plan of destruction, when he saw them repent. Jonah is heartbroken. He wanted to see the Ninevites all destroyed by God so that Israel would be free from the threat of their oppression in the future. But, Jonah knew God's heart all along.

It's a good thing Jonah wasn't God. Jonah didn't believe people would change. God did and still does. King David says: "The Lord is gracious and merciful; slow to anger and abounding in steadfast love. The Lord is good to ALL, and His mercy is over all that He has made." (Psalm 145:8-9 ESV)

That statement would certainly be true for David's relationship with God. Think about this guy who God calls,"a man after my own heart." After his affair impregnating Bathsheba and his murder of her husband Uriah, David should have not only been taken off the throne but stoned to death as well. Yet God did not allow that. As King David notes, above, God's goodness is not just directed to those of good behavior, not just to David amid his sin, but to "ALL."

The amazing thing about the Nineveh story and the King David story is that both occurred before Jesus sacrifice for all sin, for all time, was accomplished by the Cross and subsequent ressurection. That Biblical fact echos Peter's statement,"Christ, the Messiah, died for sins, once for all. The righteous for the unrighteous (the Just for the Unjust, the Innocent for the Guilty) that He might bring us to God. In His human body, He was put to death. But He was made alive in the Spirit. "(1 Peter 3:18 AMPC)

The "sins" referred to by Peter were Past, Present and Future sins. At the time of Jesus death on the cross, you and I weren't born yet. At the time of Jesus death and ressurection ALL OUR SIN WAS FUTURE. David was forgiven by Christ's death for him, even <u>before Jesus was born.</u> Thus, ALL PAST SIN IS FORGIVEN. It's hard to get my brain around, but we have to see that God exists simultaneously in the past, present, and future. I wonder if God is like the Star Trek officers who are bound by the "Prime Directive," they are not allowed to do anything that would change the past or alter the "timeline"?

But what would happen if God DID alter the timeline? Has He done so already? I believe He has. God has changed His mind already. He says "For I will be merciful to their iniquities and I will remember their sins no more."(Hebrews 8:12 ESV)

The problem is that WE remember them and our friends and relatives remember them. Oh by the way, those sins may be brought up at any time in conversation, particularly when it otherwise might look like you are having a wonderful day. The enemy also remembers them, and throws them out at us whenever it benefits him to do so. We also have Google and Facebook, which many times over will assist the enemy in his condemnation of us.

Certainly, <u>we do need to be careful of our words and behavior.</u> Not that they will affect our relationship with God, but that <u>they</u>

<u>do affect our relationships on Earth, and our witness of Christ to others</u>. As believers who have been saved by Grace, we will never be cast into Hell for what we do, say, or think. But our deeds on earth can certainly be held against us in a court of law. Our behavior can certainly result in our being disowned by our families, divorced by our spouses and demeaned on Facebook. But as far as The Lord is concerned we are O.K., simply by believing in Him and accepting his death as our death, and living our new life in Him, as he was resurrected for us. This brings us to that question that has been asked by many men and women throughout history. **"What must we do?"** We detail that history in the next chapter.

Like Eating Jelly With Chop Sticks   Jack Narvel

Chapter 11

What Must We Do to be Saved?

Many people, both in Bible history and today, have asked that question. The "Rich Young Ruler," the Pharisee in the garden with Jesus at night, and the spokesman for the group of men who had come to Pentecost while Peter was preaching. They all asked "What must we do to be saved?" Or the ancillary question,"What must we do to earn eternal Life" Notice the operative words in these questions are "<u>must do</u>," and "<u>to earn</u>." In essence these questions both implied that there was something God required us to do to "earn" His love as a reward. That was the way the Old Covenant operated, (remember Deuteronomy 28 and 29) but these folks were hoping for a different answer than "Obey the Six Hundred and Thirteen."

At Pentecost, Peter, through the leading of the Holy Spirit, must have given just the right answer to that question, because three thousand were led to the Lord that day.

All these people who asked that question, whether of Jesus or Peter, must have felt there was something more to a relationship with God than what they were experiencing. There must have been something more (or perhaps <u>less</u>) than the 613 Laws governing our relationship with God. They all asked that question."What should we do?"

When we seriously look at the relationship of God and man in the Universe, we all seek the same answer.

Hopefully, the solution to our spiritual dilemma would come by some simple action we could take that would settle that relationship "once and for all."

Well, as it turns out, that was exactly God's plan all along. Once we believe in what Jesus did for us, it's like we never acted stupidly. It's as though we never acted to disappoint God. God has changed the timeline in our favor! God changed our timeline, not only in the past, but in the future as well. Our sins that were committed are forgiven, the sins we are yet to commit are forgiven. <u>Hopefully the leading of the HolySpirit within us and our attentiveness to it, will cause us to act less stupidly than in the past.</u>

In First CorinthiansPaul reminds us,"Don't you know that you yourselves are God's temple and that God's Spirit dwells in you?" (1 Cor 3:16 ESV). That being the case, the more we are aware of that fact, the less stupidly we should act.

In Galatians Paul writes,"I have been crucified with Christ. It is no longer I who live, but Christ lives in me. And the life I now live in the flesh I live by faith in the Son of God, who loved me and gave Himself for me."(Gal 2:20 ESV)

God forgives us past present and future and He forgets our rejection of Him and His guidance in our lives. But unlike God, the PEOPLE we have offended are not so "absent-minded." Although it doesn't say so in the Bible, I have a suspicion that Uriah's relatives somehow knew David was responsible for Uriah's death. People gossip. People DO remember. In human legal matters, unless our criminal record is expunged by an appearance before a judge, any and all convictions for the violation of human law are recorded and on our record for our lifetimes. And of course, the history books, (and even Wikipedia and Google, for God's sake) perpetuate both our victories and errors for eternity, or at least until all electronic records are destroyed by a Solar Flare.

So as far as our relations to other people go, unless we apologize and make amends to Aunt Jane for wrecking her prized 1955 Buick Roadmaster, we cannot expect Aunt Jane to "forgive and forget." She might say,"I was thinking of including you and your family in my will the other day, but then I thought of the time you wrecked my Buick. 'FORGET ABOUT IT!'"

God is different than our human fathers, and Aunt Jane, however brilliant and forgiving or unforgiving they may have been. God is not like our Pastor or our Therapist. God has means at His disposal that will reconcile every broken relationship, if we allow Him. God has means that will warm and heal every broken heart. God can be the husband to the widow, the wife to the widower.

He is the One who knows everything and still chooses to love us. That is His character. He is everywhere at once. It doesn't matter where we are, dead or alive, God is always with us. Jesus even went to Hell (Sheol) and spoke to the captives there. How amazing is that? King David writes: "I see that the Lord is always with me. I will not be shaken for he is right beside me." (Psalm 16:8 ESV)

David goes even further to say, "If I ascend to Heaven, you are there. If I make my bed in Sheol, you are there."(Psalm 139:8 ESV) In life and in death, God is always with us, if we will only believe in Him.

Let's take a closer look at the Second Chapter of Acts (no, not the 1980s singing group, but the Bible, [gee whiz!]) The crowd gathered in the town square listening to Peter preach the Gospel in Acts Chapter 2. We see signs and wonders, men speaking in tongues that are foreign to them yet everyone from every nation present can understand them, as though the Apostle Peter was speaking to them in their native tongue. As Peter preached the good news of Christ given to the people of Earth by God the Father for the forgiveness of sins and for everlasting life, the people were moved in their spirits. "Now when they heard this, they were cut to the heart,(with remorse and anxiety) and they said to Peter and the rest of the apostles,'Brothers, what are we to do?'" (Acts 2:37 AMPC)

Peter replied: "Repent (change your old way of thinking turn from your sinful ways, accept and follow Jesus as the Messiah) and be baptized, each of you, in the name of Jesus Christ because of the forgiveness of your sins and you shall receive the gift of the Holy Spirit. For the promise (of the Holy Spirit) is for you and your children and to all who are far away (including the Gentiles), as many as the Lord our God calls to Himself."(Acts 2:38-39 AMPC)

What shall we do today? How can we expect to be received by this all-powerful God, who created us and the physical Universe in which we live? How can we possibly be worthy of His blessing? Not just His final Heavenly Blessing of welcoming us through the "Pearly Gates," but of the blessings He has for us here and now in our everyday earthly life. I think I've mentioned this before, but I often tell people who feel they are unworthy to accept Christ as their Savior and brother, or sister,"Jesus never cleaned any fish before He caught them."

The thief on the Cross is still the best model for today. We approach God with a lifetime of failings. We approach God full of hatred and distrust. We approach God totally broken and helpless. We say, as did the thief on the cross, "Jesus remember me when you come into your Kingdom." (Luke 23:42 ESV) We can righteously expect, today (as it was then), Jesus response to be, "Truly, I say to you, today you will be with me in Paradise."(Luke 23:43 ESV)

Now that's the Gospel. That's the Good News. It is God's grace by our faith which saves us, not our works, no matter how excellent they are. Our works will also not condemn us to Hell. Hell isn't even open yet. In Matthew we find that Hell is reserved for those who are not us."You that are accursed, depart from Me into the eternal fire prepared for the Devil and his angels." (Matt 25:41 KJV),

For those of us who are NOT angelic beings, we find that "God saved you by His grace when you believed, and you can't take credit for this; it is a gift from God." (Eph 2:8 NLT)

If you have read this far, and you still have some doubts about your self-worth, remember Abram, who was promised this blessing,"I will surely bless you, and I will surely multiply your offspring as the stars of heaven and as the sand that is on the seashore and your offspring shall possess the gate of your enemies."(Gen 22:17 ESV) Abram meant "high father," but God changed his name to Abraham, "father of a multitude" (Gen 17:5 ESV) Remember, also, that God changed Simon's name from Simon, "he has heard," to Peter, "Rock"(John 1:42 ESV).

I was in a men's group at church, at one time, where we all sought the Lord for a new name that would be His nickname for us. That may be a good exercise for you today. Ask God exactly how He sees you, and what would be His name for you. Graham Cooke says God gave him the nickname, "Gray." Be assured His name for you will lift your spirit, as you see how He sees you.

As we are held in such high esteem by our creator, why would we not believe and receive what he has for us, we brothers and sisters of Christ? God is singing,"It's a beautiful day in the Neighborhood...won't you be mine?"

In the Kingdom of Heaven (on Earth as it is in Heaven) there is no need to stand in long lines in less-than-clean places, waiting for a questionable meal and a questionable welcome. Rather, through acceptance of Jesus as our Savior, we have been predestined to receive God's blessings now and for Eternity. Our names are already written in "The Lamb's Book of Life,"from birth (Rev 21:27 NIV) They can be "blotted out" (Rev 3:5 NIV) but not if we believe in and receive in us The One who gave Himself for us, The Lord, Jesus the Christ.

Perhaps, by now, you have recognized that God had you in mind before He created the Universe. God carries your picture in His wallet. Your picture is the "Lock Screen" on His cell phone. Like the servant to whom the King gave ten Minas, ten Cities, and an additional Mina from the servant who had not used the gift the King gave him, God has incredible gifts for us. When we use them to bless others, our gifts are multiplied.

Like Eating Jelly With Chop Sticks   Jack Narvel

Like Eating Jelly With Chop Sticks — Jack Narvel

Chapter 12

The Meaning of Life - A New Commandment

I hope you have not browsed through the Table Of Contents and said to yourself, "I will skip ahead to Chapter 12; I would really just like to get the "meaning of life," without having to wade through a bunch of narrative."

For the rest of you who **have** taken the time to read the preceding chapters, I believe you will agree that this book has not just been"narrative." From this point, I will continue on with the revelations I have gotten by living through those circumstances which have been divinely placed in my path.

My six year old son, David, whom you may remember from the sledding accident (item 3, in Chapter 5), once asked me why it was that Mommy and I were smoking, as we probably knew it was harmful to us. Smart kid, good question! At the time, the kids were still in Foster Care with us. Everyone knew we intended to adopt them, but there were still legal hurdles to overcome before the adoption could be final.

I replied,"Well, David, we want to be your 'real Mommy and Daddy,' but the State of Illinois has to award us permanent custody of you so you can be our 'Real Kids'.That involves a court case and trial where everyone's opinion and evidence can be heard. We continue to smoke because the tobacco smoke has a calming effect on us. Once you are adopted and legally ours, then we will give up smoking."

He says, "But Daddy, doesn't the Bible tell us that God sees things, not just as they are on the outside, but as they are in your heart. You've said that 'in your hearts' we are already your kids and we can call you 'Mommy and Daddy'. So would it be O.K. for you to agree with God and believe that 'what is in your hearts' is already real."

O.K. then, Mister "Norman Vincent Peale," "Mister Quantum Physicist," we'll do just that! We had two cartons of cigarettes in the freezer at that time and we did not touch them for three months,(just in case we changed our minds,) then we threw them in the trash. David was wise beyond his years, but we were just learning to listen.

When we adopted David with his brother and two sisters, we had diligently studied and conversed with others who had adopted. We took classes on adoption. We had group therapy sessions.We thought we were prepared, but we really had no idea what we were in for.

If we took the kids point of view (always a good idea to take the view of others), imagine how it must feel to have the Government separate you from your family, all that you have known up to that point, regardless of how unhealthy it might have been? Were these kids whom we had chosen to adopt emotionally damaged to some degree? Yep! Were we prepared to cope with all that, times four, and solve "all their problems?" Nope! Above and beyond the psychologists and counselors the State provided, we surely needed Jesus!

There were six other couples in our "Foster Parenting" group who intended to adopt children. After a year, I asked our social worker how the other parents were doing. She said."They all have returned their children to us." WOW. I said, "Why do you think we have been successful when the others were not?" She said,"Because you don't care what other people think."

Are other people's opinions important? Certainly. But did Jesus ever give up His ministry because other people in authority disagreed with Him? Should we let the opinions of others determine what we should do? Apparently not.

What can The Word show us about dealing with others? I used to think that the "New Covenant" was doing away with the Law of Moses and adopting the belief that Jesus wanted us to do as He told the Scribe in Mark 12. The Scribe asked Jesus to tell him "Teacher, what is the greatest commandment?" Remember there were Six Hundred and Thirteen commandments. The Scribe was apparently asking Jesus for the "Reader's Digest Condensed Book" version.

Jesus was accommodating, He said,"The most important is, 'Hear O Israel: the Lord our God, the Lord is one. And you shall love the Lord with all your heart and with all your mind and with all your strength." (Mark 12:29-30 ESV)

The Scribe had not asked."O.K. then what's the second?" But Jesus goes on to reveal the second most important, "The second is this: you shall love your neighbor as yourself. There is no other commandment greater than these."(Mark 12:31-32 ESV)

When people ask me, as a Grace believer, if I think that the Old Testament commandments still apply to us? I always say,"Are you Jewish? If you are, then they probably do, but if you are a Gentile believer, then I cite Romans, Galatians, every book Paul and Peter wrote, plus Hebrews as evidence that we should be governed by "The New Covenant" and not the "Old Covenant" of Moses.

People then ask me what is this "New Covenant"? What is the Law; or what are the Laws that Jesus imparted for us to obey? Just like the Israelites in Moses time, we still ask today for the Laws of Life to live by.

We seek "Life Coaches" on-line, who can share with us the wisdom we seek. The Book of James says if we lack wisdom, we may ask God,"If any of you lacks wisdom, let him ask God, who gives generously to all without reproach, and it will be given him."(James 1:5 ESV) Or you could pay Twenty Five Dollars (or more) a month to have your coach give you advice. For me, God is my "Life Coach." He created us, He created the world we live in. What better person to ask advice than Jesus?

While Holy Spirit advice is to be sought after, it is better not to ask for more "laws to live by," our U.S. Congress has already made enough of those. The Six Hundred and Thirteen Laws of Moses were intended to convince us that we needed a Savior, not as guide for obedience which would bring peace with God. Paul characterizes the usefulness of the Law of Moses this way,"The Law was our guardian until Christ came; it protected us until we could be made right with God through faith. And now that the way of faith has come, we no longer need the Law as our guardian."(Gal 3:24-25 NLT)

Paul states in Romans 7,"At one time I lived without understanding the Law. But when I learned the command no to covet, for instance, the power of sin came to life."(Rom 7:9 NLT). Paul's natural reaction to being told "don't do it," was to "want to do it." Those of us who are parents know too well that when we tell our children,"Don't do that!" They immediately will do it, as soon as our backs are turned. The Law was never intended to correct our bad behavior, it was intended to point us toward Jesus, the Messiah, the Christ! After Jesus death and ressurection, the human race was given a New Revelation of who they were, and their purpose.

I used to quote these verses from Mark 12:29-32, Matthew 22:36-40 and Luke 10:27, and say," This is the 'New Covenant from Jesus'. Not the Six Hundred and Thirteen Laws of Moses, Moses Book of the Covenant, not even the Ten but just these two. 'Love the Lord your God with all your heart and love your neighbor as yourself.'" I felt pretty smug about saying that too!

But I had missed a key point in quoting these as the "New Covenant Laws" we need to obey. What I failed to see was that Jesus was still operating under the Law of Moses in The Four Gospels! Jesus' advice to the Scribe is NOT "New Covenant" but rather advising him how to live successfully under the "Old Covenant." Let's explore further; the Law of Moses actually contained the instruction to "Love God and love others as yourself."In Leviticus, God says to the Israelites,"Do not seek revenge or bear a grudge against anyone among your people, but love your neighbor as yourself. I am The Lord."(Lev 19:18 NIV)

Notice how the phrasing in the Old Testament is different than Jesus' in the Gospel of John. The Israelites are told not to bear a grudge "against anyone among your people." According to The Law of Moses, it was OK to hate Samaritans or Ninevites, just not the Jews. The definition of "neighbor" in the Old Testament was restricted.

However in the parable of the "Good Samaritan," Jesus went beyond those two important commands by defining who your neighbor really is. Jesus redefined what the love of others really is. Jesus had a whole new teaching that stretched beyond the

Old Covenant. It was specifically for us "New Believers," the Jews and Gentiles who came to know God after the death and ressurection of Christ.

Should we take care of our neighbor? Should we love our neighbor as we love ourselves? Here's how Jesus redefines it:

Your neighbor is not the guy who lives next door. It is not a person who agrees with you politically. Rather, Jesus says,"A new commandment I give to you, that you love one another: <u>just as I have loved you, you are also to love one another</u>." (John 13:34 ESV)

This is a radical teaching, which I have misinterpreted these many years as a Christian. Jesus did not mean, "Love one another, as you love yourself." NO, we have already investigated how many Christians <u>don't</u> love themselves, not as Jesus loved them, anyway. Many of us have self-hatred buried in our souls, which can cause illness, both physical and mental. That self hatred will surely damage our relationships with others.

As we have seen earlier in this book, self doubt and unbelief can certainly cause us to go to places where we will be insulted and so validate our feelings of low self-esteem.

How can we love our brothers in the way Jesus loves us in that "soulish" environment of today's world? In short, we can't! Jesus adjures us to go beyond our own "soulishness" to that place of "perfect love" which He has for all people.

Here's the short version of the Parable of the Good Samaritan. Check the whole story out for yourself in Luke 10:25-37:

A Jewish man was beaten up and robbed while going on a journey from Jerusalem to Jericho. As he lay by the side of the road, wounded, a Pharisee and a Priest (both Jews) passed by him, without stopping to help. They were obeying the Law of Moses because they were sworn to "do no harm."

The Priest and Pharisee did their fellow Jew "no harm" in passing him by, but they certainly did not help him either. Apparently the Priest and the Pharisee felt no compunction under the Law to help someone who was injured, even a fellow Jew. After all, there were physicians and healers who were trained to do that. If they tried to help, they might "make matters worse." Have we ever avoided getting involved in situations for that same reason?

The questions that beg here are two: (1) who is my neighbor and (2) how shall I love him? <u>Here's that remaining debt we talked about earlier that we will always owe</u>: The apostle Paul writes,"<u>Owe nothing to anyone - except for your obligation to love one another</u>. If you love your neighbor, you will fulfill the requirements of God's law." (Romans 13:8 NLT) But what kind of "love" is it? We will need to revisit this NLT translation in a few moments.

Jesus commands us to go beyond the way we have defined love in the past, even the love we have experienced from others. The love Jesus instructs us to follow is not "Philos," in the Greek, brotherly love; nor is it "Eros," the love of the flesh. Jesus commands us to stretch into the love that God has shown us.

Jesus instructs us to share totally selfless "agape" love as God shares with us. That is, love without anger, without expectation, and without conditions. In both New and Old Testament, in

Hebrews 8:12 NASB) and in Jeremiah 31:34 NASB), God says, "I will be merciful to their iniquities and I shall remember their sins no more." Remember "iniquities" are "bad stuff done on purpose," whereas sins can be unintentional, or intentional. That is far too difficult a commandment for any human being to keep. But that's for God, to abide by, not for me, isn't it?

Jesus can't really mean that we humans should forgive and love other humans as He did. Who can do that in their own human strength? How can I not only forgive, but forget that guy in High School who lied to me and stole my girlfriend? His acts were obviously intentional and intended to hurt me, while benefitting him. Can I both forgive him and forget his offense to me? I have not done so and that was over sixty years ago.

I once had a vision, during a retreat weekend, when I saw this young man (still 16 years of age in my vision) He was tied to a whipping post in the middle of what appeared to be a French Foreign Legion Outpost in the middle of a desert. I was beating him mercilessly. Then it occurred to me that while I was in this vile place, engaged in vile deeds; I was as much a prisoner of my own unforgiveness as he was. It was quite hot and uncomfortable for me, both physically and emotionally. I recognized something was amiss in my thinking.

Getting back to our kids, our adopted kids came with emotional baggage of which we had limited comprehension. We did our best to love them as we loved ourselves, we forgave them when they started fires and destroyed some of our favorite things, but, as you see by some of my stories, we have not forgotten them.

As writers, we surely must be forgiven by God for remembering the sins of others, otherwise books, movies and plays would be much less interesting than they are.

I keep getting distracted, I can't imagine why, except that this "Jesus Love" stuff is really challenging.

Getting back to the story of the good Samaritan, this man went beyond the Law of Moses. He even went beyond his cultural upbringing. He helped a Jew, the very people who were the enemies of the Samaritans. The Samaritans thought they knew who God was; the Jews KNEW that they knew who God was, but both groups had missed the point.

The "Good Samaritan" went beyond his own culture. He went beyond healing and helping. He put the injured man on his own donkey and took him to the Inn. The Samaritan not only paid two Denarii for a stay of two nights, but told the innkeeper, "Look after him' he said, 'and when I return I will reimburse you for any extra expense you may have.'"(Luke 10:25-37 NIV)

Jesus' "New Commandment" tells us that we should not only be willing to help, others, to heal others, but to actually go out of our way, to accompany them for a distance on their journey to assure that they have what they need, both physically and spiritually.

Our "neighbor" in Jesus mind, was anyone whom God puts in our path. Not just people of the same belief as you, not just people of the same country as you, not just people of the same color as you, but someone who has a need of the type of love that Jesus has given you. The driving force which should empower us to share love, as believers, is that same force that drove Jesus to "move in compassion" for others.

Let's look again at that quote from Paul earlier. I have added some clarification to it. Paul writes,"Owe no one anything, except for your obligation to love one another (as Jesus loved you). (For) if you love your neighbor,(as Jesus loved you) you will fulfill the requirements of God's Law (Jesus "New Commandment").Parentheses added are mine.(Romans 13:8 NLT)

This "New Commandment" goes beyond what I thought love should be. It goes beyond the experiences of any love which I have felt in most of my life. It's God's Perfect Love, "'agape." It is "unconditional." It transcends and transforms all things. In this New Commandment, we are being invited to participate, with God, in sharing this, His perfect love.

Are we able to share this "agape" love, on our own? No, we can't. Rather we are invited to be "co-creators" in Christ not only of a new life in ourselves, but "co-creators" of New Life in the Kingdom of Heaven, restoring others in the world in which we live today.

In that mindset of what God has done for you, and what He has placed in your heart; in this mindset of the "New Commandment" which He has given to all of us who call ourselves Christians; in this mindset of who we are in the love of God, we have our course plotted out for us. All this love of God is just "waiting to manifest" in you and I, and through you and I!

You'll remember that you are Jesus brother or sister in the Spirit. Of course, you are also His Ambassador to The Kingdom of Heaven on Earth,(2 Cor 5:18-21 NLT) and His beloved child.

Given all that the Lord has given you and all He has placed in your heart, why would you want to eat in restaurants where you are insulted by waiters? Why would you hang out with "trash-talking people" who demean you or curse you (in Chinese, or any other language for that matter)? God has so many blessings for you, salvation, inner peace, healing, prosperity in both the spirit and the physical. The Greek word for all that is "sozo." It means, according to Strong's Concordance,"to save, to keep safe and sound, to rescue from danger or destruction, to make well, to heal and restore to health."(Strong's Biblical Concordance #4982 "sozo" pronounced sode'-zo).

Why not experience it all? God will not shortchange. He has so many people who will encourage you and bless you, if you give them a chance. Why settle for less than God's best for you? It is the King's desire to bless you that you may bless many others. In First Corinthians Paul writes,"As it is written:'no eye has seen, no ear has heard, no heart has imagined, what God has prepared for those who love Him.'"(1 Cor 2:9 ESV)

For those who are still believing that we need to do some "works" to prove ourselves of value to God, I think John 6 will dispel that falsehood for you. Jesus answers the question of the men who had attended the "feeding of the five thousand" in Capernaum, on the day before. They searched for Jesus and his disciples. They wanted to perform miracles, too. When they found Him they asked,"Lord what <u>must</u> we do, to be doing the works of God?Jesus answered them,'This is the work of God, that you believe on Him whom He has sent."(John 6:28-29 ESV).

This was not the answer they were seeking. Like many of us today, we feel that we should be Billy Grahams or Mother Teresas so we may become famous for "doing the works of God!" Jesus says that's foolishness. When we are called to a work, anointed to do it and we do it, that in itself will be our reward. We don't need to be famous, just fulfilled in Christ.

When I was a "Hippie Musician" in The Bay Area, we were hired to do a New Years Eve Party at the Oakland Marina. During the break, two of the guys went outside to "smoke dope." I stayed back and suggested to the lead electric guitar player that we strike up the "Donnie Osmond version of "Deep Purple." I sang it with only the guitar accompaniment. At the end, the other band members had just walked back in as "Goon" (the guitarist) and I were receiving a "standing ovation" from the crowd. Cedric asked "What the Hell were you thinking?" I replied, "I was just taking the opportunity to be myself." I quit the group the next day. When asked why, I said,"I know who I am now and what people see in me. I don't need to be performing on stage five nights a week to prove it to myself anymore."

Whether you feel the need to perform to please other people, or perform to please God, you are acting in error. If it is not already clear from the forgoing chapters, it is NOT sin, when I do something that "excludes" God in my life for a moment. The truth is that as a believer, Jesus lives in us, so we **can't** exclude God. I had a friend who used to say that when he wanted to do something he knew was wrong, he would simply go into his "Jesus-Free Room." But as King David said, "Everywhere I go, God is there."

Frankly, it is not so much sin, when we try to avoid God, as it **is sin** when we try to "**control God**" by doing legalistic things which we think will please Him. The thought that, "If I do this then God will do that," is "Old Covenant Thinking." In fact, it is "blasphemous," today, because we are trying to "make God do something" in response to what we are doing. The "New Covenant" tells us that Jesus has already "done it all." By faith in the One who did these things for you and "as you," are you saved, not by your works. Have **faith** in what **Jesus did**.

It is **not Faith** to try to please God through **our works**. That teaching is of Buddhism and other Religions of the World. "What I do is what I get." That's "Karma" not Christianity. You don't do things for your children in the belief that they will do other things for you. e.g.: "Let's see, if I take the kids to the Zoo, then they will want to wash and wax my car." I don't think they will. They might **want** to do things for you because they know you love them **unconditionally,** but they probably won't want to "trade favors" with you. Not for very long. Kids don't want to "earn your love." As we've seen earlier in this book, a compunction to earn love out of guilt gets frustrating really quickly and can cause more anger than love.

God loves you just the way you are. As you share His unconditional love for yourself with others, you will find that other people will respond in love for Jesus and for you.

Since I've noted earlier that God has a picture of you on the "Lock Screen" of His cell phone, you may want to copy and paste this scripture to the "Lock Screen" of your phone as a reminder of your importance to Him:

Ephesians 1:4-5 (NLT):

"Even before he made the world, God loved us and chose us in Christ to be holy and without fault in his eyes. God decided in advance to adopt us into his own family by bringing us to Himself through Jesus Christ. This is what he wanted to do, and it gave Him great pleasure."

Can you believe it? Seriously <u>can you believe it?</u> You may not have believed it in the past, but I hope by now you are getting the idea that you give God great pleasure. The Word tells us that God now sees us as "Holy and without fault". Through our acceptance of Christ's death and ressurection for us and as us, we have become His beloved children. Do you believe God when He says,"you give God great pleasure"? As Earthly fathers, we experience our children, at least much of the time, as giving us "great pleasure". As Earthly fathers, we still love and delight in our kids, even when they mess up.

Even when our kids say they,"Hate us" and disrespect us on Facebook, we still love them and respect their choices, stupid as they may be at times. Why would that unlikely scenario be? Because we, like God, believe that the current circumstances of their lives are temporary. As the Apostle Paul says these are, "momentary light afflictions, which are preparing us for an eternal weight of glory beyond all comparison, as we look not to the things that are seen, but to the things that are unseen. For the things that are seen are transient, but the things that are unseen are eternal."(2 Corin 4:17-18 ESV)

This book has been about a journey of discovery into who I was created to be, in Christ. It is all about the value that I have discovered that I have to Him, and with Him living in me. I have found, often to my surprise, that I create value in others, just by being who I am. This value reflects back onto both Jesus and myself. I'm giving Him all the Honor and Glory! I hope you are discovering this Divine Value in yourself, that has been my intention. Thanks for joining me.

ADDITIONAL RESOURCES

God vs. Religion ....By Creflo Dollar
Ten Reasons to Break Free from Religious Traditions

Pure Grace ....By Clark Whitten
The Incredible Power of Unfettered Grace

The Naked Gospel ....By Andrew Farley
Truth You May Never Hear in Church

Grace Revolution ....By Joseph Prince
Experience the Power to Live Above Defeat

What Must We Do..................................By John F. Kellogg
How to Express the Holiness Both You and God Desire

Relaxing With God ....By Andrew Farley
The Neglected Spiritual Discipline

The Hyper Grace Gospel...............................By Paul Ellis
A Response to Michael Brown

I'm Saved, Now What? ....By Rick Sarver
Key Truths That Help You Experience Abundant Life

Is Sunday School Destroying Our Kids?....Sam Williamson
How Moralism Suffocates Grace

About the Author

Jack Narvel is an Ordained Minister with the Grace Fellowship International Network. He lives in Myrtle Beach, South Carolina, with his wife Jan. They both serve at Journey Church of Myrtle Beach and Grace Fellowship Int'l Network, as well as with a number of interdenominational ministries. Jack is a native of Philadelphia, Pennsylvania. He has a Masters Degree in Communication from the University of Pennsylvania.

Jack is a Vietnam Veteran. He spent five years as a hippie musician in Oakland, California, where he both sang and played a variety of percussion instruments with a band called "Jeff and Cedric James." This book was born of his experiences in life. The title of this book was the inspiration of the Holy Spirit back in 2008. The subject matter of the book was not given to him until 2018. Jack asks that we remember how long Abraham waited for God's promise to be fulfilled. "Anticipatory Patience," as Jack calls it, is a good thing. We might all use a bit more of it.

Made in the USA
Middletown, DE
07 November 2019